How to
Plant and Grow
PERENNIALS

How to
Plant and Grow
PERENNIALS

Maggie Oster

THE
APPLE
PRESS

DEDICATION

To my friends
who have stood by me
and taught me to work, love, and play

A QUINTET BOOK

Published by The Apple Press
6 Blundell Street
London, N7 9BH

ISBN 1-85076-269-4

This book was designed and produced by
Quintet Publishing Limited
6 Blundell Street
London N7 9BH

Creative Director: Terry Jeavons
Art Director: Ian Hunt
Project Editor: Judith Simons
Editor: Alison Leach
Illustrator: Rob Stone

Typeset in Great Britain by
Central Southern Typesetters, Eastbourne
Manufactured in Hong Kong by
Regent Publishing Services Limited
Printed in Hong Kong by
Leefung-Asco Printers Limited

ACKNOWLEDGMENTS

All photography by the author, Maggie
Oster, with the exception of the
following: main jacket image, Ian
Howes/Quintet Publishing; page 27;
Harry Smith Horticultural
Photographic Collection.

CONTENTS

INTRODUCTION

Billowing clouds of baby's breath, robust delphiniums reaching for the sky, translucent petals of poppies shimmering in the sun. These are a few of the images evoked by perennials in the garden. Perennials have provided generations of gardeners with a wealth of colours, shapes, textures and sizes of plants and flowers, with bloom spanning the seasons from hellebores pushing through snow in winter to the hardiest of the chrysanthemums persisting into the chilly days of autumn. With thousands of different perennial varieties available, the hardest part is narrowing the choices.

What exactly is a perennial? Basically, it is a plant that lives more than two years. As that description would also include trees and shrubs, the word is further defined as being a plant that is herbaceous, or having soft, fleshy stems that die back in the autumn. There are a few exceptions to this, such as many of the ornamental grasses, semi-woody sub-shrubs and plants with evergreen foliage. While the foliage of most perennials dies each year, the roots are able to survive varying degrees of winter cold and send up new growth in the spring. A perennial may be able to do this for several years or for decades, depending on many factors.

Besides true perennials, certain biennial plants are included in this book. Biennials take two years to complete their life cycle: in the first year from seed they produce only leaves, and in the second they grow and bloom, set seed and die.

USING PERENNIALS IN THE GARDEN

The most traditional way to use perennials is in borders, with the plants placed either in ribbonlike bands or in natural clumps. Except in very formal, geometric gardens, the latter method is generally preferred. Often, two parallel borders are developed, separated by a lawn, a path, or both. A fence, hedge or wall is often included as a backdrop. Free-standing beds, either in geometric shapes or in less formal undulating designs, are another way to use perennials in the landscape. Such beds are intended to be viewed from all sides.

The wealth of perennials available from around the world is also useful in many other ways in the landscape. A group of trees underplanted with a variety of ferns and other shade-loving perennials becomes a woodland garden. Perennials native to alpine areas or regions with

LEFT: *Free-standing beds are to be viewed from all sides and may be surrounded by lawn or paving. They may act as a divider or draw the garden visitor from one part of the garden to another.*

OPPOSITE ABOVE: *A meadow-like garden using ornamental grasses, day lilies, yarrow, geum, veronica, and black-eyed Susans turns this large expanse of lawn into a low-maintenance area.*

OPPOSITE BELOW: *Learning to combine plants successfully for a beautiful effect, such as this border of chrysanthemum, Japanese anemone, artemisia, liriope, physostegia, golden rod, asters, and other plants, means taking the time to study, plan and choose carefully.*

dry, gravelly soil are the best ones to choose in softening the harsh lines of a stone wall or making a rocky outcropping into a rock garden. A wet, marshy area beside a stream or pool turns into a bog garden when planted with perennials that tolerate very moist conditions. An open expanse of lawn is transformed into a glorious meadow garden when filled with brightly

coloured flowers and ornamental grasses that thrive in these conditions.

Perennials can also provide an accent in the landscape, or, when planted in containers, turn a terrace or patio into a flower-filled retreat.

CONSIDERING GROWING CONDITIONS

As you begin the process of deciding what perennials you want to grow, first consider your growing conditions. These factors include minimum winter temperatures, soil, light and water.

Hardiness is mainly determined by the ability of a plant to survive a minimum winter temperature. Water and soil conditions plus other factors also play a role. These work together so that even within a small garden there will be such microclimatic differences that a plant may survive in one corner but not in another. For example, temperatures will be lower at the bottom of a

hill, on the north side of a house, or in an area exposed to wind. Good drainage is a key element, for should water be allowed to collect around roots and then freeze, the results are usually fatal. With experience, you will learn which areas are best for certain plants. You may even be able to find that extra warm spot for growing a plant that is not normally hardy in your area.

Although some perennials must have full sun, there are a great number that tolerate either full sun or light shade, plus others that grow best in light or even full shade. In regions with hot, humid summers, light or partial shade is often necessary for plants to survive. This may be provided by planting on the east or west side of a building, hedge or fence so that sun is received for at least four to six hours each day. The lightly dappled shade beneath open trees is similar; this can be created by thinning out upper branches or trimming off lower ones. When choosing a lightly shaded site,

one that gets morning sun and afternoon shade is usually the best option.

Heavily dappled shade under trees, the dense shade on the north side of a building, hedge or fence, or any position with four hours or less of sun each day is considered full shade. Very few perennials bloom well in these conditions, but there are a number with beautiful foliage suitable for these areas.

For most perennials, the ideal soil, called loam, has a balanced mixture of sand, silt and clay particles, drains well, and has a generous supply of organic matter, or humus. Fortunately, organic matter can make either sandy soil that drains too quickly or clay soil that drains slowly quite amenable, because it helps to retain water and nutrients while at the same time allowing air spaces around the plant roots. An additional benefit is that it enhances the growth of soil microorganisms that release plant nutrients. The most common sources of organic matter are peat moss, compost or leaf-mould.

To determine your soil type quickly, dig up a handful of soil three to five days after a rainfall and squeeze. If it forms a ball that does not readily break apart it is probably high in clay; a loose gritty soil is mainly sand, while a soil ball that crumbles loosely is a loam. To determine drainage, dig a hole 12 in (30 cm) deep and fill with water. If the water has not seeped away in an hour, the drainage is poor. If the poor drainage is due to a clay soil, adding organic matter is usually enough,

ABOVE LEFT: *With experience you will discover that different features of your garden will have climatic variations. A bed next to a stone wall that faces south or east will be hotter in both summer and winter than other parts of the garden because of the retained and reflected heat. Such an area would be good for heat-tolerant, marginally hardy plants.*

LEFT: *For a garden with an abundance of shade there are perennial flowers and plants that will turn a dull area into one with a wealth of texture and form. A garden such as this one, planted with hostas, illustrates the many shade of green that foliage plants offer.*

but if it is due to other factors such as a hardpan, or impervious layer, beneath the top soil, then growing plants in raised beds or containers or installing drainage tiles should be considered.

Most plants grow best with an average of 1 in (2.5 cm) of rainfall or irrigation each week during the growing season. In choosing which plants to grow in your garden, consider either the natural rainfall or your willingness to supplement it. The use of a mulch helps to conserve soil moisture.

For most people, choosing plants with low-maintenance qualities is of prime importance. Some plants must be staked, others need to be divided frequently, pinched back, have faded flowers removed, be sprayed for pests, or other time-consuming chores.

DEVELOPING A DESIGN

Once you have established your growing conditions and considered the possible perennials, you are ready to develop a design. Borders are usually best if at least 4 ft (1.20 m) wide and beds at least 6 ft (1.80 m) at their widest. If there is a hedge behind a border, provide 2 ft (60 cm) of space between. A border is intended to be viewed from one, two or three sides, so place taller plants at the back with progressively shorter ones towards the front. With free-standing beds, place the tallest plants in the middle with plants of gradually

TOP: *An area shaded in the afternoon provides the ideal growing conditions for plants intolerant of heat or those that need light shade, such as this planting of hostas, astilbes, Solomon's seal, and ferns.*

ABOVE: *A quick way of determining your soil type is to pick up a handful, squeeze, then poke the soil ball with your fingers. If it crumbles easily, then you probably have the best – a loam soil.*

LEFT: *In designing a perennial border, place the taller flowers near the back, with progressively shorter flowers towards the front. Mixing in a few taller plants near the front gives the border a more dynamic look.*

decreasing heights towards the outer edges. Breaking this guideline occasionally helps to prevent monotony, and a group of tall plants in the front of a bed or border has a bold, dynamic effect. Placing some of the low-growing, spring-blooming plants toward the centre of a bed or border makes it more interesting, too.

The season of bloom and growth habit of the plants are also to be considered. Some people may be satisfied with a perennial garden that is in bloom for a specific time of the year, while others want one border to be flowering as much of the growing season as possible.

Studying the plant descriptions, and the plant chart at the back of the book, as well as observing when these plants flower in your area, will help you to coordinate and combine the plants in your garden. Generally, using smaller plants in a compact garden and larger plants in a bigger garden is recommended; this guideline is best broken when a large, strongly architectural plant is used in a small garden for a dramatic accent.

In developing flower beds and borders, do not limit yourself strictly to perennials. Combining bulbs, annuals, herbs and shrubs within a strong framework

OPPOSITE: *One of the goals in designing with perennials is to get as many months of beauty as possible. This front garden planted with masses of 'Autumn Joy' sedum, ornamental grasses, black-eyed Susan, and Russian sage provides an attractive landscape from midsummer well into winter.*

RIGHT: *Although perennials are quite wonderful enough to be used by themselves, they also combine well with other plants, including roses, shrubs, annuals, bulbs, and herbs.*

BELOW: *Monochromatic colour schemes, using shades and tints of a single colour, or analogous schemes, using adjoining colours, are calm and soothing. An example of a monochromatic scheme is black-eyed Susan planted with blackberry lily.*

of perennials will provide greater possibilities for colour, form and texture, and a longer blooming season, plus more interest in the winter months.

A beautiful, aesthetically pleasing perennial garden utilizes basic artistic design principles with regard to colour, texture, and form of flowers and foliage.

Studying a colour wheel is helpful in combining colours. Basically, remember that reds, oranges and yellows are warm colours and greens, blue and violets are cool colours, with the former implying feelings of excitement

and passion and the latter tranquillity and calm. Cool colours tend to appear farther away from the viewer, while warm colours appear closer. This effect can be used to create illusions. Cool colours planted at the back of the garden make it seem larger, while a border of warm-coloured flowers makes it seem smaller. Unfortunately, since cool colours recede, they tend to lose their impact far away and are best observed close-up. In combining warm and cool colours, warm colours are best used more sparingly as they can easily overwhelm the cooler-coloured flowers.

In developing colour schemes, it is helpful to understand that a pure colour is called a hue, a tint is lighter, and a shade is darker. There are four basic colour schemes. Monochromatic schemes utilize flowers in various tints and shades of one colour. In a garden, green is always present, so a truly monochromatic garden is not possible. Analogous schemes usually utilize the tints and shades of three adjoining colours on the colour wheel, such as yellow, yellow-orange and orange. Complementary schemes combine colours that are opposite on the colour wheel, such as orange and blue or yellow and violet. These are difficult to achieve successfully, but by using pure hues, including white flowers or foliage, and intermingling plants, they can

LEFT: *Complementary colour schemes utilize colours opposite on the colour wheel, with the most popular combination being purple and yellow, such as this bed of catmint, yarrow, knapweed and pinks.*

OPPOSITE: *Polychromatic colour schemes, using all the colours available, is a challenge to do well.*

BELOW: *Plant form and texture are two other important considerations besides colour when designing with perennials. Repeating these is one way to strengthen the garden design. The open, spreading 'Ruby Glow' and 'Autumn Joy' sedums with medium-textured foliage is offset by the spiky, fine-textured blue fescue and coarser-textured yucca.*

be very powerful. Polychromatic schemes combine any and every colour; the result can be garish or pleasing.

Plant form is another important design consideration. The five basic forms of perennials are rounded, vertical, open, upright and spreading, and prostrate. Beds and borders may be composed of only one form, the repetition of several forms, combinations of complementary forms, or a mixture of all the forms.

Texture refers to the appearance of the plant, not to actually how it feels to the touch. The terms fine, medium, and coarse are determined by the size and density of the foliage and flowers. As with colour, spatial illusions can be created with texture. Plants with coarse texture appear closer, and fine-textured ones seem further away. Coarse-textured plants at the back of the garden make the garden seem smaller, and fine-textured ones in a narrow border make it appear wider.

Once you have analyzed your site, considered the design basics, and made a list of plants you want to include, you are ready to draw a garden plan. Drawing a plan to scale on graph paper will help you to get a sense of the space and proportions as well as the number of plants needed. Determine the dimensions of the site and outline the shape of the bed or border on the graph paper. From your list of plants, begin drawing in the clumps of plants on a sheet of tracing paper laid over the graph paper; include as many of the plant characteristics, usually in code, as needed to help you to have an

Although this process may seem tedious, by carefully choosing plants suited for your area, your garden, and your preferences rather than just buying at random will give you a much better chance of having a breathtaking garden for many years to come.

PREPARING THE SOIL

Since the perennial garden is intended to bring lasting pleasure, adequate preparation of the soil before planting is worth every bit of effort. If the area is large or you are unfamiliar with the pH and nutrient levels in your garden, have the soil tested at a laboratory or use one of the simple soil test kits that are available from garden centres.

Soil can be damaged by digging when it is too wet, so wait until it is partially dry. Remove any large stones and compost the sod. For best results, use a spade or fork to turn the soil over to a depth of 12–18 in (30–45 cm); alternatively, rototill the soil as deeply as possible. Spread a 2–3-in (5–7.5-cm) layer of organic matter evenly on top. Sprinkle on lime to adjust pH, according to soil test recommendations, and granular or timed-release fertilizer, again according to test recommendations or directions on the package label. An average recommendation is 3–5 lb (2.5–2.25 kg) of a phosphorus-rich fertilizer or 10 lb (4.5 kg) of commercially dried cow or sheep manure per 100 square ft (9 sq m).

ABOVE: *Many perennials are long-lived, so it is important to prepare the soil well. Remove rocks and compost the sod. With a spade, fork, or rototiller, work the soil at least 8 in (20 cm) deep, then incorporate a layer of organic matter and the recommended amount of fertilizer.*

accurate picture of the garden. For example, you might want information about height, form, colour and season of bloom. Overlaying layers of tracing paper can help in experimenting with different combinations or seeing how the garden will look at different seasons. Use coloured pencils or markers to indicate colours, if desired. Unless the garden is very small, placing at least three of the same plants together gives the greatest impact.

RIGHT: *Perennials bought locally at a garden centre or nursery may be growing in 4-inch (10-cm) or larger pots. Choosing plants locally allows you to see first-hand the quality and appearance of the plants.*

Using a spade or rototiller, work these ingredients into the soil. Rake the surface smooth.

BUYING AND PLANTING PERENNIALS

Perennial plants may be purchased locally at garden centres and nurseries, usually in 4-in (10-cm) or 1-gallon (3.75-litre) pots. Most of these plants will be old enough to bloom the first year. Select plants that are bushy and compact, with healthy green foliage and no sign of insects or diseases.

There are a great number of mail-order companies offering seed, while others ship young seedling plants, dormant bare-root plants, or older, larger plants in pots. Some companies are specialists in rare and unusual varieties. Many have colourful catalogues filled with detailed facts about the different plants, providing a valuable source of information. Most companies are reliable, but if you have never ordered by mail before, talk with other gardeners to learn about their experiences. Spring catalogues are mailed in the middle of winter. Plants ordered then will be shipped in early spring as dormant bare-root plants, or later in containers.

If possible, plant on a day that is cool and cloudy, with rain predicted in a day or so. Planting in late afternoon is better than in the morning. Avoid hot or windy weather.

When planting dormant bare-root perennials, the roots should not dry out, so place small stakes at the proper spacings in the prepared soil, and unwrap and plant each one individually. With a trowel dig a hole large enough so the roots spread out. Except as noted in the Encyclopedia Section, set the point where the roots meet the stem or crown at ground level. Fill in with soil around the roots and tamp gently. Then water thoroughly.

Although container-grown plants can be planted at any time they are purchased during the growing season, planting in spring after the last frost is preferred. Rather than using stakes to mark planting spots, you can set the pots out and move them around until satisfied. When ready to plant, dig a hole, gently remove the plant from the pot, loosen the roots slightly with your fingers or cut them with a knife if they are very thick, and set into the hole. The soil level should be just slightly higher than in the pot, as the plant will settle. Then water thoroughly.

ABOVE: *Plants growing in containers can be planted almost any time during the growing season. Prepare the soil and dig a hole large enough for the roots to spread out easily. Gently remove the plant from the pot, loosen the roots, and set the plant in the hole at the same depth as in the pot. Fill in with soil around the roots, tamp gently, and water well.*

FERTILIZING

A complete fertilizer contains nitrogen, phosphorus, and potassium. The percentage of these elements, always in the order above, is described by the three numbers on the package, such as 5–10–10. Most perennials grown for their blooms do best with a fertilizer lower in nitrogen than the other two elements, as nitrogen benefits foliage growth at the expense of flowers. Fertilizer may be applied in granular form, timed-release pellets, or as a liquid.

Additional fertilizer is not necessary in the first year of planting if the area is well-prepared, although a light feeding in midsummer would be all right. In subsequent years, feed once in the spring with about 2 lb (1 kg) of a phosphorus–rich fertilizer per 100 square ft (9 sq m) and again in midsummer. Liquid fertilizers are especially good for spot feeding those plants that are heavy feeders or those that seem to need an extra boost.

ABOVE: *Mulching with a several-inch (centimetre) layer of organic material, such as this partially composted ground bark and tree limbs, is beneficial in several ways. It helps the soil to retain moisture for longer, reduces the need for watering, deters weeds, keeps the soil cool, and adds vital organic material to the soil.*

WATERING

Although most perennials tolerate average soil, or one that briefly dries out, a great many perennials thrive in a soil that remains evenly moist but is never soggy. If natural rainfall does not provide this, supplemental watering is necessary.

The best method is to use a rubber, plastic, or canvas soaker hose laid among the plants. Water in the morning so the foliage has a chance to dry off before nightfall, as dampness encourages the spread of disease organisms. Soak the soil thoroughly; it should be moist 3–4 in (7.5–10 cm) deep.

WEEDING AND MULCHING

Weeds are inevitable in any garden. Try to pull them while they are still young before they get deep roots or flower and set seed. Try not to disturb the roots of the perennials. If a large clump of soil is removed when weeding, bring in additional topsoil from another part of the garden.

Adding a layer of organic mulch helps to keep weeds in check. It also slows down the evaporation of moisture from the soil, keeps the soil cool, which encourages root growth, and adds humus to the soil as it decomposes. In spring after removing any weeds, apply a layer of mulch several inches (centimetres) thick over the surface of beds and borders, tapering it thinly near the perennials. Some of the possible organic mulches include partly decayed leaves, rotted compost, chopped bracken, bark chippings, straw, spent hops, moistened peat, lawn mowings and well-decayed manure.

STAKING

There are two types of staking needs: for the tall, single-stalked plants, such as delphinium, foxglove and monkshood, and for plants with thin, floppy stems, such as yarrow, aster, chrysanthemum and coreopsis.

Use bamboo stakes or wooden poles for the tall plants, inserting each one 12 in (30 cm) into the ground and 1 in (2.5 cm) from the stalk. Use a plant tie or twine to attach the stalk to the stake loosely. If the tie is too tight, the plant will be injured.

Bushy, thin-stemmed plants can be staked with any of several types of purchased supports or by encircling the plant with twiggy tree branches 18–24 in (45–60

ABOVE: *Stake single-stemmed tall plants, such as delphinium, with bamboo, wood, or metal stakes set 1 ft (30 cm) deep and tied loosely to the plant at several points along the stem.*

ABOVE: *Plants with many thin stems can be supported by surrounding the plants with twiggy tree branches in spring.*

cm) long. When the plant is half that height, insert several branches into the soil around the plant. As the season progresses, the foliage will hide the twigs.

PINCHING, THINNING, AND DISBUDDING

Pinching out the growing tip from a plant forces side branches to grow more readily, making plants shorter, sturdier, bushier and with more flowers. Use your fingers to remove a small amount of the growth. This is usually done several times before the beginning of July. Chrysanthemums need this treatment but other perennials such as phlox and asters benefit as well.

Some perennials including phlox, delphiniums, sneezewort, Shasta daisies and asters, produce so many shoots that growth is spindly and air circulation is poor, which promotes fungus diseases. Thinning out some of the stalks when growth is 4–6 in (10–15 cm) tall will reduce this problem.

Disbudding, or removing some of the flower buds, allows the remaining bud to produce an extra large flower. Remove the small side buds early in development, if desired, on such plants as peonies, hibiscus and large-flowered chrysanthemums.

DEADHEADING

A relatively self-explanatory term, deadheading refers to cutting off the dead, or faded, flowers. This not only makes the garden neater and cleaner, but also prevents seed development. This is often desirable because seed development can weaken the plant, cause it to stop blooming, or allow it to re-seed and become a nuisance. Often, the seedlings are of inferior quality to the parent, especially if the latter is a hybrid or other cultivar. With some early-blooming plants, such as lupin, phlox, camomile and delphinium, removing the faded flowers makes the plants bloom again in late summer or autumn.

WINTER PROTECTION

After several frosts have killed back plants, cut off the dead stems to 2–4 in (5–10 cm). Removing this debris

ABOVE: *Removing faded flowers and spent stems keeps the garden looking attractive, often encourages reblooming, and reduces the places pests can overwinter. Foliage and stems that are not diseased can be composted, which can then be used to enrich the soil or serve as a mulch.*

from the garden not only makes it look more attractive during the winter, but it also reduces the places where pests can overwinter.

A winter mulch protects tender plants and prevents shallow-rooted perennials from being heaved out of the ground through alternate freezing and thawing of the soil. To apply, wait until the ground has frozen to a depth of 2 in (5 cm) and plants are completely dormant. Then, spread a 3–6-in (7.5–1.5-cm) layer of loose, open mulch, such as oak leaves, light pine branches or straw around plants. This layer can be thicker for extra-tender perennials.

CONTROLLING PESTS AND DISEASES

Pests seldom become a serious problem with the great majority of perennials, especially if preventative measures are taken. These include:

■ fertilizing and watering regularly so plants are vigorous and healthy and not stressed;
■ growing varieties that are resistant to pests;
■ picking off bugs and dropping them into a can of petrol;
■ using natural controls such as birds, toads, ladybirds and other creatures that eat insects;
■ catching earwigs and slugs by laying boards in the garden at night and destroying them in the morning;
■ checking plants regularly and treating for any pest at the first sign;
■ removing and destroying dead or distressed foliage or flowers from the garden throughout the growing season;
■ cleaning up thoroughly in the autumn so pests will have fewer places to overwinter in the garden.

If insects or disease do become a serious problem, use a pesticide, following the manufacturer's recommendations. The best organic controls for most insects are insecticidal soaps, pyrethrum and rotenone; for caterpillars, use *Bacillus thuringiensis*. The two safest broad-spectrum chemical controls are carbaryl and malathion. For fungus diseases, use either benomyl or sulphur. There is no solution for virus diseases except to destroy the plant and control the aphids or leafhoppers that spread the disease.

Leaf miners are insects that tunnel through leaf tissue, leaving white trails which disfigure the plant but do not affect its health. They are best controlled by removing and burning the damaged foliage.

Control powdery mildew with fungicide applications or by thinning out growth to improve air circulation around plants and keeping the soil moist during summer. Avoid wetting the foliage when watering.

STARTING PERENNIALS FROM SEED

Most gardeners either buy their perennials from local or mail-order nurseries or get plants from other gardeners. Starting perennials from seed is much less usual, except for certain plants that readily grow this way. These include English daisy, delphiniums, pinks, hibiscus, foxgloves, gloriosa daisies, lupins, Shasta daisy and painted daisy.

The procedure is much the same as starting annual seeds indoors or in a greenhouse, except that there is often a two-year wait before the plants bloom. This long lag time necessitates developing a nursery area for growing the plants until they can be in the garden as well as protecting them during the winter.

Perennials have differing germination requirements, so follow the instructions on the seed packet. Use any of the specialized equipment for starting seeds, such as peat moss cubes or pellets or peat pots, plastic pots, trays, cell-packs filled with moistened seed compost. Sow the seeds, then handle according to the specific requirements on the packet. Some perennial seeds must have heat or light to germinate, while others need cool temperatures or darkness. Sometimes the seed coats must have special treatment, such as being nicked with a file or having boiling water poured over them. The germination time varies greatly as well. Whatever the procedure, be sure to keep the growing medium moist. Once the seeds germinate, provide bright, indirect light, either by growing under fluorescent lights, or placing in a greenhouse.

After several sets of leaves have developed, transplant the seedlings to larger pots or into a nursery bed. Shelter them with cloches or continue growing in a cool greenhouse or indoors under lights for several weeks until they are actively growing again. At this time, transplant to a nursery area outdoors. Water and feed regularly during the summer. Mulch the nursery bed in late autumn after the ground has frozen or cover with a cold frame.

ABOVE: *When dividing perennials, use a large, fork to dig up the entire clump, then use your hands to pull the clump into smaller pieces.*

DIVIDING PERENNIALS

As perennials spread and grow, each plant competes with itself and other plants for water, nutrients, and space. Dividing perennials, then, is a significant part of their upkeep. Division is needed either to rejuvenate an aging plant, to control the size of a plant or to have additional plants.

Spring- and summer-blooming plants are generally divided in late summer or autumn and autumn-blooming plants in early spring. In areas with winters of −20°F (−28°C) or colder, division is often best accomplished in the spring, so plants have a full growing season to become established before facing the rigours of winter; the exception are the plants blooming in early spring, such as primroses, leopard's bane and lungwort.

Several days previously, water the bed well. For spring division, plan on keeping two to four buds or sprouts with each section; when dividing in autumn or whenever in active growth, cut the plants back by half and keep at least two to four stems with each portion.

With a large fork or spade, dig up the entire clump. If possible, use your hands to divide the clump into smaller sections. When roots are tightly ensnarled, insert two large forks back to back in the center and press the handles toward each other, prising the clump apart. For plants with thick, carrot-like roots, use a knife to cut apart each section. If the centre of the clump has not died, it is sometimes possible to use a spade to cut away portions at the outer edges of the plant.

Replenish the soil in the hole from which the clump was removed with top soil, organic matter, and a handful of a nitrogen–free fertilizer. Replant one or more of the divisions in the hole, if desired, and replant the others in another part of the garden, share them with friends, or throw them away. Keep the plants well watered until established again.

PROPAGATING PERENNIALS FROM STEM AND ROOT CUTTINGS

Using stem cuttings for propagation is an efficient way to get additional plants without digging up the parent plant. Generally, spring is the best time to take stem cuttings of summer-blooming plants, and early summer is best for plants blooming in spring and autumn.

To take a cutting, cut a piece 4–8 in (10–20 cm) long from the top of a stalk. It is best to cut slightly below the point where leaves join the stem. Remove the lower leaves, moisten the stem end, dip in rooting hormone, and put in a pot of moistened seed compost. Insert a label showing the date and the name of the plant, and cover the pot with a plastic bag. Place in a warm spot with bright, indirect light. Do not let the seed compost dry out; mist the cuttings several times a day. When cuttings have rooted and new growth starts, transplant to bigger pots or to a nursery bed. When plants are large enough, transfer to the garden.

Root cuttings are mainly useful when a large number of plants are wanted. It works best with just a few perennials. In early spring, either cut off some of the outer roots without disturbing the plant or dig up the entire plant and cut up all or part of the roots.

For plants with fine roots, such as phlox, yarrow, sea holly, spurge, blanket flower, salvia and Stokes' aster, cut the roots into pieces 2 in (5 cm) long and spread them horizontally over the surface of a tray of moistened potting compost. Cover them with ½ in (12 mm) more of moist compost. Keep moist until the sprouts develop, then treat the plants as seedlings.

For plants with fleshy roots, such as bee balm, bleeding heart, baby's breath, poppies and peonies, cut the roots into pieces 2–3 in (5–7.5 cm) long, keeping the top ends facing the same direction. Plant them vertically, top ends up, in moistened potting compost with ¼ in (6 mm) sticking above the soil. Keep moist until sprouts develop, then treat as seedlings.

SPECIAL USES, SITES, AND CHARACTERISTICS

PERENNIALS FOR CUT FLOWERS

Achillea YARROW
Aconitum MONKSHOOD
Adenophora LADYBELLS
Alchemilla LADY'S MANTLE
Amsonia BLUE STARS
Anchusa BUGLOSS
Anemone ANEMONE
Anthemis CAMOMILE
Aquilegia COLUMBINE
Asclepias BUTTERFLY WEED
Aster ASTER
Astilbe ASTILBE
Baptisia FALSE INDIGO
Bergenia BERGENIA
Campanula BELLFLOWER
Centaurea KNAPWEED
Centranthus RED VALERIAN
Chrysanthemum CHRYSANTHEMUM
Cimicifuga SNAKEROOT,
    BUGBANE
Clematis CLEMATIS
Coreopsis TICKSEED
Delphinium LARKSPUR
Dianthus CARNATION, PINKS
Dicentra BLEEDING HEART
Dictamnus BURNING BUSH
Digitalis FOXGLOVE
Doronicum LEOPARD'S BANE
Echinacea PURPLE CONE FLOWER
Echinops GLOBE THISTLE
Erigeron FLEABANE
Eryngium SEA HOLLY
Eupatorium MIST FLOWER,
    JOE-PYE WEED
Filipendula QUEEN-OF-THE-PRAIRIE,
    MEADOW SWEET, DROPWORT
Gaillardia BLANKET FLOWER
Geum GEUM
Gypsophila BABY'S BREATH
Helenium SNEEZEWEED
Heliopsis FALSE SUNFLOWER
Helleborus HELLEBORE
Hesperis SWEET ROCKET
Heuchera CORAL BELLS
Hosta PLANTAIN LILY
Iris IRIS
Kniphofia TORCH LILY
Lavandula LAVENDER
Liatris GAYFEATHER
Lobelia CARDINAL FLOWER,
    GREAT BLUE LOBELIA
Lupinus LUPIN

Lychnis MALTESE CROSS,
    GERMAN CATCHFLY, ROSE CAMPION
Lysimachia JAPANESE
    LOOSESTRIFE
Macleaya PLUME POPPY
Monarda BEE BALM
Ornamental grasses
Paeonia PEONY
Papaver ORIENTAL POPPY
Phlox PHLOX
Physostegia OBEDIENT PLANT
Platycodon BALLOON FLOWER
Primula PRIMROSE
Rudbeckia CONEFLOWER
Salvia SALVIA
Scabiosa SCABIOUS
Sedum STONECROP
Solidago GOLDEN ROD
Stokesia STOKES' ASTER
Thalictrum MEADOW RUE
Thermopsis CAROLINA THERMOPSIS
Veronica SPEEDWELL
Viola VIOLET

PERENNIALS FOR BOG GARDENS

Aruncus GOAT'S BEARD
Astilbe ASTILBE
Cimicifigua SNAKEROOT
Eupatorium JOE-PYE WEED
Ferns SENSITIVE, ROYAL AND
    CINNAMON FERNS
Filipendula QUEEN-OF-THE-PRAIRIE,
    MEADOW SWEET
Helenium SNEEZEWEED
Hibiscus ROSE MALLOW
Iris (selected varieties) IRIS
Lobelia CARDINAL FLOWER
Lysimachia LOOSESTRIFE
Lythrum PURPLE LOOSESTRIFE
Monarda BEE BALM
Physostegia OBEDIENT PLANT
Primula japonica JAPANESE
    PRIMROSE

PERENNIALS FOR ROCK GARDENS

Alchemilla LADY'S MANTLE
Aquilegia COLUMBINE
Arabis ROCK CRESS
Armeria THRIFT
Artemisia schmidtiana
    SILVER MOUND
Asarum WILD GINGER
Aubrietia PURPLE ROCK CRESS
Aurinia GOLD DUST
Bellis COMMON DAISY
Bergenia BERGENIA
Campanula (selected varieties)
    BELLFLOWER
Cerastium SNOW-IN-SUMMER
Dianthus PINKS
Dicentra (selected varieties)
    BLEEDING HEART
Filipendula vulgaris DROPWORT
Gaillardia 'Goblin'
    BLANKET FLOWER
Galium SWEET WOODRUFF
Geranium CRANE'S-BILL
Geum GEUM
Heuchera CORAL BELLS
Hosta (selected varietes)
    PLANTAIN LILY
Iberis CANDYTUFT
Iris (selected varieties) IRIS
Lavandula LAVENDER
Linum FLAX
Phlox (selected varieties) PHLOX
Primula PRIMROSE
Sedum (selected varieties)
    STONECROP
Stachys BIG BETONY
Veronica (selected varieties)
    SPEEDWELL
Viola VIOLET

PERENNIALS FOR FRAGRANCE

Centranthus RED VALERIAN
Cimicifuga SNAKEROOT, BUGBANE
Dianthus CARNATION, PINKS
Dictamnus BURNING BUSH
Filipendula MEADOW SWEET,
    QUEEN-OF-THE-PRAIRIE
Galium SWEET WOODRUFF
Hemerocallis (selected
    varieties) DAY LILY
Hesperis SWEET ROCKET
Hosta plantaginea FRAGRANT
    PLANTAIN LILY
Iris BEARDED IRIS
Lavandula LAVENDER
Monarda BEE BALM
Oenothera EVENING PRIMROSE
Paeonia PEONY
Phlox paniculata GARDEN PHLOX
Primula (selected varieties)
    PRIMROSE

PERENNIALS FOR DRIED FLOWERS

Achillea YARROW
Alchemilla LADY'S MANTLE
Anaphalis PEARL EVERLASTING
Artemisia MUGWORT, WORMWOOD,
    SOUTHERNWOOD
Asclepias BUTTERFLY WEED
Belamcanda BLACKBERRY LILY
Cimicifuga SNAKEROOT, BUGBANE
Dictamnus BURNING BUSH
Echinacea PURPLE CONE FLOWER
Echinops GLOBE THISTLE
Eryngium SEA HOLLY
Gypsophila BABY'S BREATH
Helenium SNEEZEWEED
Heliopsis FALSE SUNFLOWER
Lavandula LAVENDER
Liatris GAYFEATHER
Macleaya PLUME POPPY
Oenothera EVENING PRIMROSE
Ornamental grasses
Rudbeckia CONEFLOWER
Salvia SALVIA
Scabiosa SCABIOUS
Sedum STONECROP
Solidago GOLDEN ROD

SPECIAL USES, SITES, AND CHARACTERISTICS

PERENNIALS TO ATTRACT BUTTERFLIES

Aquilegia COLUMBINE
Asclepias BUTTERFLY WEED
Campanula BELLFLOWER
Centaurea macrocephala GOLDEN KNAPWEED
Centranthus RED VALERIAN
Delphinium LARKSPUR
Dianthus CARNATION, PINKS
Digitalis FOXGLOVE
Echinacea PURPLE CONE FLOWER
Echinops GLOBE THISTLE
Eupatorium MIST FLOWER, JO-PYE WEED
Hemerocallis DAY LILY
Hesperis SWEET ROCKET
Heuchera CORAL BELLS
Iris BEARDED IRIS
Kniphofia TORCH LILY
Liatris GAYFEATHER
Lobelia CARDINAL FLOWER
Lupinus LUPIN
Lychnis ROSE CAMPION
Lythrum PURPLE LOOSETRIFE
Monarda BEE BALM
Nepeta CATMINT
Papaver ORIENTAL POPPY
Phlox PHLOX
Rudbeckia CONEFLOWER
Salvia SALVIA
Stachys BIG BETONY

PERENNIALS FOR MEADOW GARDENS

Achillea YARROW
Amsonia BLUE STARS
Anthemis CAMOMILE
Asclepias BUTTERFLY WEED
Aster ASTER
Baptisia FALSE INDIGO
Coreopsis TICKSEED
Echinacea PURPLE CONE FLOWER
Echinops GLOBE THISTLE
Erigeron FLEABANE
Eryngium SEA HOLLY
Eupatorium coelestinum MIST FLOWER
Gaillardia BLANKET FLOWER
Helenium SNEEZEWEED
Heliopsis FALSE SUNFLOWER
Hemerocallis DAY LILY
Liatris GAYFEATHER
Linum FLAX
Lobelia CARDINAL FLOWER, GREAT BLUE LOBELIA
Lychnis GERMAN CATCHFLY, ROSE CAMPION
Lysimachia LOOSESTRIFE
Lythrum PURPLE LOOSESTRIFE
Monarda BEE BALM
Oenothera EVENING PRIMROSE
Ornamental grasses
Physostegia OBEDIENT PLANT
Rudbeckia CONEFLOWER
Solidago GOLDEN ROD
Thermopsis CAROLINA THERMOPSIS

PERENNIALS FOR GROUND COVERS

Alchemilla LADY'S MANTLE
Arabis ROCK CRESS
Armeria THRIFT
Asarum WILD GINGER
Aubrietia PURPLE ROCKCRESS
Aurinia GOLD DUST
Bergenia BERGENIA
Brunnera SIBERIAN BUGLOSS
Campanula (selected varieties) BELLFLOWER
Cerastium SNOW-IN-SUMMER
Chrysogonum GOLDEN STAR
Dianthus PINKS
Ferns
Geranium CRANE'S-BILL
Galium SWEET WOODRUFF
Gypsophila repens CREEPING BABY'S BREATH
Heuchera CORAL BELLS
Hosta PLANTAIN LILY
Iberis CANDYTUFT
Ornamental grass BLUE FESCUE
Phlox subulata CREEPING PHLOX
Stachys LAMB'S TONGUE

LOW-MAINTENANCE PERENNIALS

Achillea YARROW
Aconitum MONKSHOOD
Alchemilla LADY'S MANTLE
Amsonia BLUE STARS
Artemisia ARTEMISIA
Aruncus GOAT'S BEARD
Asclepias BUTTERFLY WEED
Astilbe ASTILBE
Aurinia GOLD DUST
Baptisia FALSE INDIGO
Bergenia BERGENIA
Brunnera SIBERIAN BUGLOSS
Campanula BELLFLOWER
Centaurea KNAPWEED
Chrysanthemum coccineum PYRETHRUM
Cimicifuga SNAKEROOT
Clematis CLEMATIS
Coreopsis TICKWEED
Dicentra BLEEDING HEART
Dictamnus BURNING BUSH
Doronicum LEOPARD'S BANE
Echinacea PURPLE CONE FLOWER
Echinops GLOBE THISTLE
Erigeron FLEABANE
Eryngium SEA HOLLY
Euphorbia SPURGE
Filipendula QUEEN-OF-THE-PRAIRIE, MEADOW SWEET, DROPWORT
Geranium CRANE'S-BILL
Gypsophila BABY'S BREATH
Helenium SNEEZEWEED
Heliopsis FALSE SUNFLOWER
Helleborus HELLEBORE
Hemerocallis DAY LILY
Heuchera CORAL BELLS
Hibiscus ROSE MALLOW
Hosta PLANTAIN LILY
Iberis CANDYTUFT
Iris sibirica SIBERIAN IRIS
Liatris GAYFEATHER
Linum FLAX
Lychnis ROSE CAMPION
Lysimachia LOOSESTRIFE
Lythrum PURPLE LOOSESTRIFE
Mertensia VIRGINIA COWSLIP
Nepeta CATMINT
Oenothera missouriensis EVENING PRIMROSE
Ornamental grasses
Paeonia PEONY
Papaver ORIENTAL POPPY
Physostegia OBEDIENT PLANT
Platycodon BALLOON FLOWER
Polygonatum SOLOMON'S SEAL
Pulmonaria LUNGWORT
Rudbeckia CONEFLOWER
Salvia superba VIOLET SAGE
Scabiosa SCABIOUS
Sedum STONECROP
Solidago GOLDEN ROD
Stachys BIG BETONY
Stokesia STOKES' ASTER
Thalictrum MEADOW RUE
Thermopsis CAROLINA THERMOPSIS
Tradescantia SPIDERWORT
Veronica SPEEDWELL

ENCYCLOPEDIA SECTION

THE PERENNIALS CHOSEN for this book are ones that have been favourites for generations as well as those that have only recently come into garden use. Besides popularity, the length of time each year the plant makes an aesthetic contribution to the garden was also considered. A plant should either bloom for a long period or be attractive for most of the the growing season. Conversely, if the foliage does become unattractive, then it should die down quickly so other plants fill in.

In this era of stress-filled lives, gardening should be a source of relaxation, not just another chore on an endless list. Maintenance, then, is of key importance. Some of the old-fashioned perennials require a lot of care but are so beloved that they are still widely grown. More and more, however, gardeners are choosing plants that have as many low-maintenance characteristics as possible. These include resistance to insects and diseases; tolerance of a wide range of soil types and moisture conditions; infrequent need for division (preferably no more than every four years); resistance to summer heat; and infrequent need for staking.

Few plants meet all of these criteria, but ones that satisfy as many as possible have been included in the following section. Another attribute was hardiness; with only a few exceptions, the plants described are hardy to at least −30°F (−34°C). Conversely, most of the plants can also be grown in areas with much warmer winter temperatures, except subtropical regions.

DEFINING BOTANICAL TERMS

Both the common and the botanical, or Latin binomial, names have been used in the plant descriptions. Just as a person's full name is necessary for proper identification, the same applies to plants. A common name for a plant in one region may be used for an entirely different plant somewhere else while Latin names are the same throughout the world.

A binomial includes the generic name, which is followed by the species name. Sometimes there is a third word, which is a subspecies or variety (var.) name.

OPPOSITE *Salvia* x *superba* 'MAY NIGHT'

Taxonomists sometimes change botanical names, and the older forms have been included for clarification. A garden form, sport, clone, or result of a hybrid cross is called a cultivar; the cultivar name is enclosed in single quotation marks. Cultivars are usually propagated vegetatively, from divisions or cuttings, as they may or may not reproduce true from seed.

GUIDE TO USING THE ENCYCLOPEDIA SECTION

■ Perennials are arranged alphabetically by their botanical, or Latin binomial name.
■ Below each entry is a chart of symbols that provide easy reference to information on specific temperature and positioning needs, or to plants which are recommended for particular sites or uses.
■ Information relating to colour, height, bloom time, soil, sun and spacing requirements for all the perennials featured in this section is tabulated for easy reference in the chart at the back of the book.

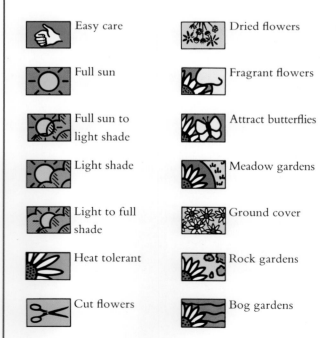

Easy care	Dried flowers
Full sun	Fragrant flowers
Full sun to light shade	Attract butterflies
Light shade	Meadow gardens
Light to full shade	Ground cover
Heat tolerant	Rock gardens
Cut flowers	Bog gardens

ACHILLEA

ACHILLEA

YARROW

CERTAIN YARROWS ARE indispensable to any garden where low maintenance is a consideration. The pungently scented, feathery, grey or dark green leaves are topped with flat flower clusters for a month or more from early to midsummer, and longer if faded flowers are removed. In shades of yellow, red, pink and white, all yarrow flowers are good for cutting and using either fresh or dried.

■ **SPECIES, VARIETIES AND CULTIVARS** There are numerous cultivars and hybrids of varying heights of the golden, or fernleaf, yarrow (*Achillea filipendulina*). *A.* × *taygetea* grows 18 in (45 cm) tall with silvery leaves and pale yellow flowers.

Common yarrow (*A. millefolium*), also known as milfoil, is a weedy plant with off-white flowers, but selected forms with pink to red flowers are better for the garden and are good cut flowers. Plants grow 18–24 in (45–60 cm) tall with flowers 2–3 in (5–7.5 cm) across. The cultivars 'Fire King', 'Cerise Queen' and 'Kelwayi' make good border plants.

Achillea filipendulina 'CORONATION GOLD'

A number of the new hybrid yarrows usually grow 2 ft (60 cm) tall, with broad clusters of 4-in (10-cm) flower heads. The white-flowered sneezewort (*A. ptarmica*) can be invasive and needs division every other year, but the flowers are good for cutting. Low-growing *A. tomentosa* is a rapid grower best suited to large rock gardens or as an edging.

■ **CULTIVATION AND CARE TIPS.** Yarrows grow best in full sun with average or poor, well-drained soil. If grown in rich, moist soil, they tend to become invasive. Space larger-growing types 12–18 in (30–45 cm) apart and shorter ones 10–12 in (25–30 cm) apart, either singly or in groups of three. The taller varieties may need staking. Divide every fourth year. All are hardy to −50°F (−46°C).

■ **PROPAGATION.** Division in spring, keeping four or five young shoots with each portion. Seed.

■ **PESTS AND DISEASES.** Basically trouble-free, but crown gall, mildew, or rust may occur.

Achillea millefolium 'FIRE KING'

Adenophora confusa

MONKSHOOD

Magnificently elegant monkshoods have much to recommend them: attractive glossy, divided foliage; wonderful spikes of unusually hooded blue flowers in late summer and early autumn that are good for cutting and a long life.

Although used medicinally, all plant parts are poisonous and care should be taken with small children.

■ **SPECIES, VARIETIES AND CULTIVARS.** Azure monkshood (*Aconitum carmichaelii*, sometimes listed by its old name *A. fischeri*) grows about 3 ft (90 cm) tall. Hardy to −40°F (−40°C). *A. × cammarum* (also listed as *A. napellus*) has more finely divided leaves with blue to violet flowers on 3–4-ft (90-cm–1.2-m) stems in mid to late summer. Hardy to −20°F (−28°C).

■ **CULTIVATION AND CARE TIPS.** Such lushness requires a humus-rich, slightly acidic soil that is moist and well-drained. Regular watering in summer is necessary. Plants do best in cool to moderate climates but grow in hotter climates in light shade. A summer mulch in all climates is beneficial. Staking is advisable. Cut back spent flower stems to encourage growth. Plant as individual specimens 18 in (45 cm) from other plants and in the middle to back of a border.

■ **PROPAGATION.** Division in fall or early spring, if necessary. Seed.

■ **PESTS AND DISEASES.** Seldom bothered, but crown rot, mildew, mosaic, or wilt may occur.

Aconitum carmichaelii

LADYBELLS

Resembling their close relatives, the campanulas, ladybells have delicate, ¾-in (18-mm), blue or purple bell-like flowers from mid to late summer on long-lived plants growing 2–3 ft (60–90 cm) tall.

■ **SPECIES, VARIETIES AND CULTIVARS.** China-native *A. confusa* is generally shorter while the European *A. lilifolia* is slightly taller with paler, fragrant flowers.

■ **CULTIVATION AND CARE TIPS.** They grow in sun or light shade with a humus-rich, moist, well-drained soil. They do not transplant readily. Group several plants together about 12 in (30 cm) apart for greatest effect. Hardy to −40°F (−40°C).

■ **PROPAGATION.** Seed. Cuttings.

■ **PESTS AND DISEASES.** Seldom bothered.

Alchemilla mollis

ALCHEMILLA

LADY'S MANTLE

THE SPREADING MOUNDS of velvety, rounded grey-green leaves with fan-like pleats and serrated edges have made lady's mantle a favourite for the front of a border. The frothy masses of chartreuse flowers lasting several weeks in early summer are delightful in fresh or dried bouquets. Sold variously as *Alchemilla mollis* or *A. vulgaris*, plants grow 12 in (30 cm) tall with the flower stems extending 6 in (15 cm) above.

■ **CULTIVATION AND CARE TIPS.** They prefer partial shade, but full sun is tolerated in climates with cool summers. In mild-winter areas, the plants are evergreen. Moist, well-drained, humus-rich soil is needed. Plants readily reseed, so remove faded flowers if new plants are not wanted. Plants seldom need to be divided, but can be after the fourth year if desired. Plant in groups of three, spaced 12 in (30 cm) apart or use mass plantings as a ground cover. Hardy to −40°F (−40°C).

■ **PROPAGATION.** Division in spring or autumn.

■ **PESTS AND DISEASES.** Seldom bothered.

AMSONIA

BLUE STARS

THIS LOW MAINTENANCE perennial has loose, rounded clusters of pale blue, ½-in (12-mm), star-shaped flowers on stiff 2–3-ft (60–90-cm) stems that provide a gentle contrast to other stronger-coloured flowers in spring and early summer. They are good for cutting if the stems are seared in a flame to prevent 'bleeding'. The narrow, glossy, willow-like leaves remain attractive all season long before turning yellow in the autumn. The most readily available species is *A. tabernaemontana*.

■ **CULTIVATION AND CARE TIPS.** They grow in average moist or dry soil in full sun or light shade. Adding humus to the soil and mulching will encourage best growth, but don't overfertilize or growth will be too open. Plants form clumps 18–24 in (45–60 cm) wide and should be planted singly or in small groups 18 in (45 cm) apart towards the middle of a border. Hardy to −40°F (−40°C).

■ **PROPAGATION.** Division in spring. Seed.

■ **PESTS AND DISEASES.** Seldom bothered.

Amsonia tabernaemontana

Anaphalis cinnamomea

ANAPHALIS

PEARL EVERLASTING

THROUGHOUT SUMMER small clusters of pearly white flowers on 2-ft (60-cm) stems provide material for dried flower arrangements. Cut when the flowers just begin to show their centres, first putting in a vase of water for several hours, then hanging upside down in a dark, dry place. It is one of the few silver- or grey-foliaged plants able to grow in moist soil.

■ **SPECIES, VARIETIES AND CULTIVARS.** *Anaphalis triplinervis* forms 12–18-in (30–45-cm) mounds of spear-shaped grey leaves that become greener when the plant blooms. *A. cinnamomea* (also listed as *A. yedoen-*

sis) has narrower leaves and woolly stems. It is a better choice for dry soils.

■ **CULTIVATION AND CARE TIPS.** They grow best in moist but well-drained soil in full sun to light shade. Plant as single specimens or in groups of three, spacing 12 in (30 cm) apart. Hardy to −40°F (−40°C).

■ **PROPAGATION.** Division in spring, usually every four years.

■ **PESTS AND DISEASES.** Seldom bothered.

Anchusa azurea

BUGLOSS, ALKANET

RESEMBLING FORGET-ME-NOTS, bugloss is favoured for the airy sprays of intensely coloured, dark blue flowers in bloom over a long period in summer. There are a number of varieties of *Anchusa azurea*.

■ **CULTIVATION AND CARE TIPS.** They prefer deep, humus-rich, well-drained soil with full sun or very light shade. Cutting back after flowering encourages a second blooming. The coarse, hairy foliage may flop unless staked. Plants do not live very long but self-sow readily. Division is needed every two to three years. Plant singly or in groups of three near the back of a border, spacing plants 18 in (45 cm) apart. Hardy to −40°F (−40°C).

■ **PROPAGATION.** Division or root cuttings in spring or autumn. Seed.

■ **PESTS AND DISEASES.** Leafhoppers; mosaic.

ANEMONE

JAPANESE ANEMONE, VINE-LEAVED ANEMONE

ANEMONES ARE A diverse group of plants, including both perennials and bulbs, with some best suited for woodland or rock gardens.

■ **SPECIES, VARIETIES AND CULTIVARS.** The autumn-blooming varieties of Japanese anemone (*A.* × *hybrida*, also called *A. hupehensis* var. *japonica*) and vine-leaved anemone (*A. vitifolia* or *A. tomentosa* 'Robustissima') are some of the most handsome perennials for the garden. The flowers are in shades of pink or white on slender, swaying, 2–3-ft (60–90-cm) branched stems above 2-ft (60-cm) mounds of deeply lobed, dark green leaves. The vine-leaved anemone blooms a month earlier and is an excellent plant naturalized among shrubs. Of the spring-flowering anemones, the pasque flower (*A. pulsatilla*, also known as *Pulsatilla vulgaris*) has unusual, fern-like leaves covered with silken white hairs and fuzzy seed heads. Plants grow 8–12 in (20–30 cm) tall. Hardy to −30°F (−34°C). The snowdrop anemone (*A. sylvestris*) blooms a little later in spring with fragrant white flowers on 12-in (30-cm) plants.

■ **CULTIVATION AND CARE TIPS.** Autumn-blooming anemones must have partial shade or full sun in a location out of wind and a humus-rich soil that is moist in summer but well-drained. The vine-leaved anemone is slightly more tolerant of heat, cold, sun and dry soil. Hardy to −20°F (−28°C), plants develop slowly even with ideal conditions, but they are long-lived and should not be moved. A loose winter mulch of straw, oak leaves or evergreen branches is recommended for Japanese anemones. They are best when planted in groups of three, spaced 18 in (45 cm) apart. Spring-blooming anemones need full sun to partial shade with well-drained soil and self-sow readily, spaced 8 in (20 cm) apart. Hardy to −30°F (−34°C). Snowdrop anemones grow in partial shade with humus-rich, well-drained soil. Hardy to −40°F (−40°C).

■ **PROPAGATION.** Root cuttings or division in autumn.

■ **PESTS AND DISEASES.** Flea beetles; caterpillars; aphids; slugs; mosaic; rust.

Anemone x *hybrida* 'SEPTEMBER CHARM'

Anthemis tinctoria 'KELWAYI'

ANTHEMIS
CAMOMILE

SUNNY YELLOW DAISY-LIKE flowers excellent for cutting, ferny aromatic foliage, a tolerance of hot, dry conditions and sandy, slightly alkaline soil are the advantages of ox-eye camomiles (*Anthemis tinctoria*).

■ **SPECIES, VARIETIES AND CULTIVARS.** *A. marschalliana* (also called *A. biebersteiniana*) forms dense 10-in (25-cm) tall mats of feathery, silver foliage perfect for the rock garden. Plant 12 in (30 cm) apart. Hardy to −30°F (−34°C). St John's camomile (*A. sanctijohannis*) is similar to ox-eye camomile but has bright orange flowers and grey-green leaves. Also an excellent cut flower. Hardy to −20°F (−28°C).

■ **CULTIVATION AND CARE TIPS.** Plants tend to develop dead areas in the centre and must be divided every other year or so. Staking may be necessary with the 2-ft (60-cm) plants. Grow in full sun in average, well-drained soil, spacing plants 15 in (38 cm) apart. Deadhead regularly to prolong blooming.

■ **PROPAGATION.** Division in spring. Seed.

■ **PESTS AND DISEASES.** Seldom bothered except by mildew when air circulation is poor.

COLUMBINE

THESE OLD FAVOURITES deserve garden space for their unusually shaped early summer flowers. The cup and spur may be the same colour or in contrasting colours. Good for cutting, the flowers may be double.

■ **SPECIES, VARIETIES AND CULTIVARS.** 'McKana's' hybrids have become one of the most popular strains since their introduction. There is an extensive colour range of large flowers with sturdy growth 30–36 in (75–90 cm) tall. Especially notable is the Japanese fan columbine (*Aquilegia flabellata*) with its bright blue flowers with spurs curving prominently inwards and the fan-shaped, grey-blue leaves on the 15-in (38-cm) plants. Its dwarf and white-flowered forms grow 8–12 in (20–30 cm) tall.

■ **CULTIVATION AND CARE TIPS.** These graceful plants are useful in sunny perennial plantings in cooler summer climates, but generally they do best in lightly shaded borders and woodlands. The shorter types are excellent for rock gardens. Well-drained but not overly dry soil is a must. Plants readily self-sow. Set plants 12 in (30 cm) apart. Hardy to −40°F (−40°C).

■ **PROPAGATION.** Seed.

■ **PESTS AND DISEASES.** Leaf miners; aphids; leaf spot; rust; mosaic.

Aquilegia flabellata 'NANA'

Arabis caucasica

ARABIS

ROCK CRESS

Aₗₜₕₒᵤ₉ₕ ᵣₒ꜀ₖ ꜀ᵣₑₛₛₑₛ are usually grown in the rock garden, two species are also of particular merit as an edging or accent plant along walls, banks, or other landscape features.

■ **SPECIES, VARIETIES AND CULTIVARS.** Creeping 8-in (20-cm) mounds of soft grey-green leaves mark *Arabis caucasica*, while *A. procurrens* forms a compact mat of tiny, glossy evergreen leaves. Both bear loose spikes of ½-in (12-mm), fragrant white flowers in spring.

■ **CULTIVATION AND CARE TIPS.** They must have loose, well-drained, limy soil of only average fertility and full sun. Cut back the flowers after blooming. Set plants 8–12 in (20–30 cm) apart. Hardy to −40°F (−40°C).

■ **PROPAGATION.** Division in spring. Seed.

■ **PESTS AND DISEASES.** Gall midge; club root; white blister; downy mildew. Will rot in hot, humid summers.

32

ARMERIA

THRIFT, SEA PINK

NEAT, GRASSLIKE CLUMPS of evergreen leaves bear leafless stalks with pink or white 1-in (2.5-cm), globe-shaped flower heads in spring and early summer. Thrifts are excellent for the rock garden, between flagstones, along walls, or at the front of a border.

■ **SPECIES, VARIETIES AND CULTIVARS.** A few of the varieties of the 6-in (15-cm) *Armeria maritima* are worth considering, such as the white 'Alba', cherry red 'Dusseldorf Pride', the intense red 'Bloodstone', and the deep pink 'Vindictive'. Plantain thrift (*A. pseudo-*

armeria, or *A. plantaginea*) forms more strapping clumps to 18 in (45 cm) tall but still with narrow leaves.

■ **CULTIVATION AND CARE TIPS.** They must have average to sandy, well-drained soil in full sun. Set plants 8–12 in (20–30 cm) apart. Divide every three years. Deadhead regularly. Hardy to −40°F (−40°C).

■ **PROPAGATION.** Division in spring. Seed. Basal cuttings in late summer.

■ **PESTS AND DISEASES.** Seldom bothered.

Armeria maritima

Aruncus dioicus

ARTEMISIA

MUGWORT, WORMWOOD, SOUTHERNWOOD

THESE SILVER- OR grey-leaved plants are mostly grown for the effect of the foliage. Only white mugwort, *Artemisia lactiflora*, is grown for its masses of tiny, creamy white, fragrant blooms, borne on 4–6-ft (1.20–1.80-m) tall plants in midsummer.

■ **SPECIES, VARIETIES AND CULTIVARS.** Avoid common mugwort (*A. vulgaris*) and Roman wormwood (*A. pontica*) because both are highly invasive. Among the most widely sought of silver-foliaged plants is *A. schmidtiana* 'Silver Mound'. The feathery 12-in (30-cm) mounds spread up to 18 in (45 cm) across. Trimming plants back before they flower lessens the tendency to open in the middle. Plants may also rot in hot, humid climates. Southernwood (*A. abrotanum*) and wormwood (*A. absinthium*) grow 18–24 in (45–60 cm) tall with finely divided grey leaves. Both dry readily for flower arrangements and wreaths as well as use in moth repellent bags. Beach wormwood (*A. stelleriana*) is a tough, adaptable plant; it grows 12–18 in (30–45 cm) tall.

■ **CULTIVATION AND CARE TIPS.** They grow easily in full sun in dry, well-drained soils. Set plants 1–2 ft (30–60 cm) apart. Hardy to −30°F (−34°C).

■ **PROPAGATION.** Division in spring. Cuttings.

■ **PESTS AND DISEASES.** Aphids; rust.

Artemisia absinthium 'LAMBROOK SILVER'

ARUNCUS

GOAT'S BEARD

DESERVING TO BE more widely grown, goat's beard (*Aruncus dioicus*, also known as *A. sylvester*) is a handsome, large, shrubby plant for the back of a border, the centre of a bed, among shrubs, in a wildflower garden or beside a pool. Plants grow 3 ft (90 cm) or more across and 5 ft (1.5 m) or taller with magnificent creamy white, feathery clusters of tiny flowers in early summer. The leaves are segmented and stems branch readily. The variety 'Kneiffi' has small, narrow leaves, giving it a delicately textured appearance, and only grows 2–3 ft (60–90 cm) tall.

■ **CULTIVATION AND CARE TIPS.** Long-lived, they grow best in partial shade and tolerate a wide range of soil conditions, but prefer a humus-rich, moist soil. Plants will tolerate full sun if soil is kept consistently moist. Plants seldom need staking, neither are they invasive. Set plants 24–30 in (60–75 cm) apart. Cut the stems off to several inches (cm) tall in the autumn. Hardy to −30°F (−34°C).

■ **PROPAGATION.** Although sometimes difficult and seldom needed, division in spring or autumn, if desired. Seed.

■ **PESTS AND DISEASES.** Seldom bothered, except by sawflies or occasionally caterpillars in spring.

Asarum europaeum

ASARUM
WILD GINGER

FORMING A DENSE MAT of shiny, heart-shaped leaves 6 in (15 cm) tall, European wild ginger (*A. europaeum*) is an excellent ground cover for fully to partially shaded areas. In areas with milder winters, the glossy foliage remains evergreen. Wild ginger derives the name from the aromatic scent of the foliage and roots when crushed. It is seldom invasive. In spring, purple-brown, bell-shaped flowers 1 in (2.5 cm) or less across bloom at ground level. A wild ginger native to North America (*A. canadense*) has dull green, deciduous leaves.

■ **CULTIVATION AND CARE TIPS.** Besides shade, they must have moist, well-drained, humus-rich soil to grow well. Set plants 8–12 in (20–30 cm) apart and 1 in (2.5 cm) deep. Hardy to −20°F (−28°C).

■ **PROPAGATION.** Division in spring.

■ **PESTS AND DISEASES.** Seldom bothered except where slugs and snails are a problem.

ASCLEPIAS
BUTTERFLY WEED

THE BRIGHT ORANGE, red, or yellow clusters of flowers in midsummer are true to their name, butterfly weed (*Asclepias tuberosa*). These long-lived, easy-care plants are related to the milkweeds, and in the autumn they form similar canoe-shaped pods that are useful in dried arrangements. Butterfly weed can be used as a cut flower, but the stems must be seared in a candle flame to stop the milky sap from flowing. Stocky-stemmed with long, narrow, bristly leaves, the plants grow 2–3 ft (60–90 cm) tall with the clusters of stems branching towards the top. They are very variable as to flower shade and blooming time.

■ **CULTIVATION AND CARE TIPS.** Drought-tolerant due to its taproot, it grows best in almost any sandy to average well-drained soil in full sun. Plants are slow to emerge in the spring, so mark their location well. Plant 12 in (30 cm) apart in the spring or autumn when the plant is dormant, setting the taproot vertically with the point where the stems emerge 1–2 in (2.5–5 cm) below the soil surface. Hardy to −40°F (−40°C).

■ **PROPAGATION.** Seed. Division or root cuttings in early spring.

■ **PESTS AND DISEASES.** Seldom bothered.

Asclepias tuberosa

Aster x *frikartii*

ASTER

ASTER, MICHAELMAS DAISY

ASTERS ARE AN indispensable part of the summer and autumn garden, with the most popular garden forms growing 1–6 ft (30 cm–1.80 m) tall. All have daisy-like flowers, usually with yellow centres and blue, lavender, purple, pink, red or white petals.

■ **SPECIES, VARIETIES AND CULTIVARS.** *Aster × frikartii* is considered one of the best perennials. The open bushes grow 2–3 ft (60–90 cm) tall with fragrant, 2–3-in (5–7.5-cm) lavender blue flowers produced over a long period in summer and autumn; these are excellent cut flowers. Although hardy to −20°F (−28°C), mulching with evergreen branches is necessary in areas with −10°F (−23°C) or colder temperatures and soil must be well-drained. Tolerant of wet soils, the Michaelmas daisy (*A. novae-angliae*) has hairy, grey-green leaves and forms large clumps with stiff, woody stems growing 3–6 ft (90 cm–1.8 m) tall. Long-blooming during the autumn, the deep purple flowers are 1–2 in (2.5–5 cm) across and close at night. *A. novi-belgii* and its many hybrids usually grow 1–4 ft (30 cm–1.2 m) tall. Plants bloom during autumn and make excellent cut flowers. In areas with a long growing season, pinch out the growing tips twice by midsummer to make plants bushy. Stake taller varieties.

■ **CULTIVATION AND CARE TIPS.** They do best in full sun in moist but well-drained soil that is average to humus-rich. Mulch in late spring to retain soil moisture and water during droughts. Deadhead regularly as plants readily self-sow but do not stay true to type and can become weedy. Cut stems when flowering is over in autumn. Stake tall-growing varieties. Set plants 12–18 in (30–45 cm) apart. Asters do not grow well in hot, semi-tropical coastal climates. Most varieties hardy to −30°F (−34°C).

■ **PROPAGATION.** Division every other year is necessary in spring or autumn with most hybrids. Cuttings. Seed.

■ **PESTS AND DISEASES.** Tarsonemid mites; powdery mildew; root rot; wilt; slugs; caterpillars.

Astilbe x *arendsii* 'PEACH BLOSSOM'

ASTILBE

ASTILBE

ASTILBES ARE ONE OF the most favoured, easily grown and long-lived perennials for shaded areas. Most plants have neat clumps of segmented, dark green leaves. Depending on the cultivar, flowering is from early to late summer. The feathery spires of tiny flowers in shades of pink, red, rose, and white may be used for cutting.

■ **SPECIES, VARIETIES AND CULTIVARS.** A group of hybrids, *Astilbe* × *arendsii* is the most widely available. Most of the cultivars grow 2–3 ft (60–90 cm) tall with dark green or reddish foliage. The creeping *A. chinensis* 'Pumila' forms a dense mat with magenta-pink flowers growing 12 in (30 cm) tall, and is excellent for rock gardens or the front of a border. *A. taquetii* 'Superba' grows 3–4 ft (90 cm–1.2 m) tall with broad, bronze-green leaves and tall, narrow spires of magenta-pink flowers; it is the last astilbe to bloom and is the most heat- and drought-tolerant type.

■ **CULTIVATION AND CARE TIPS.** They prefer partial shade with moist but well-drained, humus-rich soil and extra fertilization. In cooler climates, full sun is acceptable. Plant 12–18 in (30–45 cm) apart. Cut back in late autumn or early spring. Hardy to −30°F (−34°C).

■ **PROPAGATION.** Division in early spring every three years yields largest growth and best flowers.

■ **PESTS AND DISEASES.** Seldom bothered.

PURPLE ROCK CRESS

A SPLENDID STAPLE of the spring garden, purple rock cress (*Aubrietia deltoidea*) is in its glory used at the front of a border, tumbling out of a stone wall, in a rock garden or among flagstones. Forming 6-in (15-cm) tall mats of downy, grey-green leaves that spread to 12 in (30 cm) or more across, the ½-in (12-mm) or larger flowers may be purple, rose, red or lavender, depending on the cultivar.

■ **CULTIVATION AND CARE TIPS.** It thrives in full sun but tolerates partial shade and needs sandy, well-drained soil containing lime and a cool, moist climate for best growth. In areas with hot summers, plants are short-lived. Shear the plants back after flowering, except ones in walls, which should just be deadheaded. Space 6–8 in (15–20 cm) apart. Hardy to −20°F (−28°C).

■ **PROPAGATION.** Division in autumn. Cuttings in autumn and overwintered in a greenhouse. Seed.

■ **PESTS AND DISEASES.** White blister; mildew.

Aubrietia deltoidea

AURINIA

GOLD DUST

THE GOLDEN SUNSHINE of spring seems to have come to earth in gold dust, *Aurinia saxatilis* (also known as *Alyssum saxatile*). Easily grown, the dense, 12-in (30-cm) mounds of hairy grey-green leaves are covered with tiny, bright yellow flowers in early spring. Used as an edging to paths or steps, at the front of a border, in a rock garden, or spilling over stone walls, it is a perfect accompaniment to spring bulbs. Besides the species, there are varieties with variegated leaves, double flowers, dwarf growth, and flowers in various shades of yellow.

■ **CULTIVATION AND CARE TIPS.** For best growth, they need full sun and poor to average to sandy, very well-drained soil. Do not fertilize as rich soil causes plants to be open and sprawling. Plants may be short-lived in areas with hot, humid summers. Shear plants by one-third to one-half after flowering to encourage compact new growth. Space plants 8–12 in (20–30 cm) apart. Hardy to −30°F (−34°C).

■ **PROPAGATION.** Division in spring. Cuttings in summer. Seed.

■ **PESTS AND DISEASES.** Slugs; flea beetles; downy mildew; white blister. If club root kills feeder roots, plants must be dug up and destroyed.

Aurinia saxatilis

Baptisia australis

BAPTISIA
FALSE INDIGO

A LUSH, ELEGANT, shrubby plant, false indigo (*B. australis*) has sturdy, upright, 3–4-ft (90 cm–1.2 m) branching stems with blue-green leaves and pea-like, 1-in (2.5-cm), deep blue flowers. After blooming in early summer, the seed pods are also attractive, and both flowers and seed pods are good for cutting.

■ **CULTIVATION AND CARE TIPS.** Long-lived and never invasive, it is somewhat difficult to transplant so choose its location well. Tolerant of dry soil because of its taproot, it grows in full sun to partial shade in average to humus-rich, well-drained soil. Space plants 2 ft (60 cm) apart. Hardy to −40°F (−40°C).

■ **PROPAGATION.** Sow seed outdoors as soon as ripened or in the spring.

■ **PESTS AND DISEASES.** Seldom bothered.

BELAMCANDA
BLACKBERRY LILY

T HE IRIS-LIKE PLANTS of blackberry lily (*B. chinensis*) grow 30 in (75 cm) tall. In midsummer thin, branching stalks bear clusters of 2-in (5-cm), yellow-orange flowers marked with red-purple dots. Fading flowers form seed pods that open to reveal shiny black seeds resembling blackberries; these are good for dried arrangements. Plants readily self-sow, but seedlings are easily pulled if not wanted. *B. flabellata*, grows 12 in (30 cm) tall and has yellow, unspeckled flowers.

■ **CULTIVATION AND CARE TIPS.** Readily growing in full sun to partial shade and tolerating average to humus-rich, well-drained soils, set plants 1 in (2.5 cm) deep and 12 in (30 cm) apart. Use as a specimen in the middle of a border. Plants are long-lived and dividing is seldom necessary. Hardy to −20°F (−28°C).

■ **PROPAGATION.** Seed. Division of rhizomes in spring or autumn.

■ **PESTS AND DISEASES.** Seldom bothered, except very occasionally by iris borers.

Belamcanda chinensis

Bellis perennis

BELLIS

COMMON DAISY

THE COMMON DAISY (*B. perennis*) is often grown as a biennial. It is a perennial nonetheless and beloved as a spring- and early-summer accent for the border or rock garden. There are many varieties, with the 1–2-in (2.5–5-cm) flowers in shades of red, rose, pink, and white, and either as singles or doubles. Most types grow 3–6 in (7.5–15 cm) tall with the flower stalks emerging from the crown of dark green leaves.

■ **CULTIVATION AND CARE TIPS.** It grows well in sun and tolerates partial shade. A humus-rich, moist but well-drained soil is best. Space plants 6 in (15 cm) apart. Hardy to −40°F (−40°C), but plants need a winter mulch in areas with −20°F (−28°C) and colder.

■ **PROPAGATION.** Division every year in early autumn. Seeds sown outdoors in late spring for bloom the following year or started indoors in midwinter.

■ **PESTS AND DISEASES.** Seldom bothered.

BERGENIA

BERGENIA

GROWN BOTH FOR ITS foliage and its spring-blooming flowers, bergenia can be used at the front of flower beds and borders, massed along paths, or used as a ground cover under shrubs and trees. The cabbage-like leaves are often evergreen, sometimes turning bronze in winter, and are used in flower arrangements. The clusters of small pink, magenta or white flowers are borne on thick, leafless stalks, which should be removed when flowers fade. Plants grow 12 in (30 cm) tall and as wide, spreading slowly by creeping rhizomes.

■ **SPECIES, VARIETIES AND CULTIVARS.** The two most widely grown species are the heart-leaved bergenia (*Bergenia cordifolia*) and the slightly smaller, winter-blooming bergenia (*B. crassifolia*). There are a number of excellent hybrid cultivars available.

■ **CULTIVATION AND CARE TIPS.** They grow well in light shade in hotter climates or in full sun in cooler areas and if soil is kept moist; otherwise they tolerate a wide range of soil types. Richer soil will require plants to be divided every three to four years. Space plants 12 in (30 cm) apart. A winter mulch may be beneficial in areas with lows of −20°F (−28°C) and colder.

■ **PROPAGATION.** Division in spring or autumn, with each start having a 3–4-in (7.5–10-cm) piece of rhizome. Seed.

■ **PESTS AND DISEASES.** Leaf spot.

Bergenia 'ABENDGLUT' ('EVENING GLOW')

SIBERIAN BUGLOSS

ROUGH, HEART-SHAPED leaves and blue forget-me-not-like flowers in spring make this a useful, low-maintenance, long-lived specimen plant in a border or rock garden or as a ground cover under trees and shrubs. The neat clumps grow 12–18 in (30–45 cm) tall. Named varieties of *Brunnera macrophylla* (also listed as *Anchusa myosotidiflora*) are available, including variegated-leaf forms. These must be propagated by division; they will not come true to seed. Remove any solid green leaves from variegated types or they will take over.

■ **CULTIVATION AND CARE TIPS.** Although tolerant of full sun and a wide range of soils, it does best in humus-rich, moist but well-drained soil in partial shade. Remove faded flowering stems, or leave if self-seeding is desired. Space plants 12 in (30 cm) apart. Hardy to −40°F (−40°C).

■ **PROPAGATION.** Seldom necessary, but division is possible in spring or autumn. Seed.

■ **PESTS AND DISEASES.** Seldom bothered.

Brunnera macrophylla

BELLFLOWER

AN INVALUABLE GROUP of perennials, the bellflowers offer an amazing assortment of plant sizes and shapes for use in beds, borders, walls and rock gardens. The predominant flower colour is blue, although white, pink, and purple forms exist. The taller types make excellent cut flowers. Most types look best when planted in groups of three. Deadhead regularly. A loose mulch of oak leaves or evergreen branches will help to protect plant crowns from winter injury.

■ **SPECIES, VARIETIES AND CULTIVARS.** Carpathian harebell (*Campanula carpatica*) grows 8–12 in (20–30 cm) tall, forming broad, trailing clumps of small heart-shaped leaves. The 1–2-in (2.5–5-cm) violet-blue or white cup-shaped flowers bloom throughout summer on wiry stems. Plant 10 in (25 cm) apart. Start from seed or divide in spring. Hardy to −40°F (−40°C). Clustered bellflower (*C. glomerata*) grows 1–3 ft (30–90 cm) tall with clusters of 1-in (2.5-cm) purple or white flowers at the ends of erect stems from early to midsummer. Foliage is coarse and hairy. Space plants 2 ft (60 cm) apart, and divide every other year. Tolerant of wet soil. Plants may become invasive when grown in shade. Hardy to −40°F (−40°C). Milky bellflower (*C. lactiflora*) grows 3–5 ft (90 cm–1.5 m) tall with pale blue, violet blue, pink, or white 1-in (2.5-cm), bell-shaped flowers borne on long stiff spikes in summer. Staking may be necessary. One of the easiest bellflowers to grow, space plants 12–18 in (30–45 cm) apart. Hardy to −20°F (−28°C).

Giant bellflower (*C. latifolia*) forms bold clumps of rough leaves and grows 3–4 ft (90 cm–1.2 m) tall but does not usually need staking. It is more tolerant of light shade and moist soil than most bellflowers. The 2-in (5-cm) summer-blooming flowers are purple-blue or white. Plants readily self-sow. Hardy to −30°F (−34°C). The biennial Canterbury bells (*C. medium*) and its popular cup-and-saucer form, *C. m.* var. *calycanthema*, are the showiest bellflowers. The summer-blooming 2–3-in (5–7.5-cm) flowers may be single or double, and white, purple, blue, or pink on stems 15–30 in (38–75 cm) tall. Set plants 12 in (30 cm) apart. Hardy to −30°F (−34°C). Peach-leaved bellflower (*C. persici-*

Campanula lactiflora

folia) forms clumps of narrow leaves with 2–3 ft (60–90 cm) tall flower spikes. There are numerous cultivars with 1–2-in (2.5–5-cm) flowers in shades of blue or white and either single or double bells. Divide plants in spring every two or three years, setting plants 18 in (45 cm) apart. If desired, allow to naturalize in the garden. Hardy to −30°F (−34°C). Serbian bellflower (*C. poscharskyana*) is a vigorous, drought-tolerant, spreading plant forming large 6–12-in (15–30-cm) tall mats with abundant 1-in (2.5-cm), bell-shaped lavender-blue flowers throughout summer. It may become invasive. Divide in spring or grow from seed, setting plants 12 in (30 cm) apart. Hardy to −40°F (−40°C). Harebells (*C. rotundifolia*), also known as bluebells in Scotland, form dainty tufts 6–12 in (15–30 cm) tall. The slender flower stems bear lavender-blue or white 1-in (2.5-cm), bell-shaped flowers throughout summer. Plants can readily self-sow. Divide in spring or start from seed, setting plants 8–12 in (20–30 cm) apart. Hardy to −40°F (−40°C).

■ **CULTIVATION AND CARE TIPS.** Generally, they are easily grown and quite adaptable. Unless otherwise noted, they thrive not only in full sun but also in light shade, especially in hot climates. The preferable soil is humus-rich and moist but well-drained. Most types look best when planted in groups of three. Deadhead regularly for recurrent blooming. A loose mulch of oak leaves or evergreen branches will help to protect plant crowns from winter injury.

■ **PROPAGATION.** Plant seed of biennial types every year. Species can be started from seed. Most named varieties must be propagated from cuttings or division in spring, as they do not usually come true from seed. Most bellflowers need dividing only every third or fourth year, if at all.

■ **PESTS AND DISEASES.** Slugs; snails; froghoppers; wilt. Rust on Carpathian, milky, and peach-leaved bellflowers. Leaf spot on Canterbury bells and peach-leaved bellflower. Crown rot if water is allowed to stand around roots.

Campanula medium

Centaurea macrocephala

CENTAUREA

KNAPWEED, CORNFLOWER

THREE SPECIES are particularly eye-catching additions to the perennial garden and tolerant of neglect as well. Each has strongly coloured, thistle-like or fringed flowers that are excellent for cutting.

■ **SPECIES, VARIETIES AND CULTIVARS.** Persian cornflower (*Centaurea hypoleuca*, also listed as *C. dealbata*) blooms over a long period at the height of summer with 2-in (5-cm) vivid red-violet flowers centred with white. Spreading rapidly, plants grow 2 ft (60 cm) tall with coarsely cut leaves, dark green above and downy white beneath. Hardy to −40°F (−40°C). Attracting butterflies, golden knapweed (*C. macrocephala*) blooms for a short period in midsummer, bearing 3-in (7.5-cm) bright yellow flowers that are useful cut, fresh or dried. The bold 4-ft (1.2-m) plants have large, coarse leaves and make a good specimen plant. Hardy to −40°F

(−40°C). Knapweed or Montana cornflowers (*C. montana*) have 3-in (7.5-cm), deep violet-blue flowers in late spring and early summer. White and dark pink varieties are available. Plants grow 2 ft (60 cm) tall with downy, silver-grey leaves, and spread rapidly by self-sowing and underground stems. This is an excellent plant for a meadow garden or as a filler among early flowers. Hardy to −30°F (−34°C).

■ **CULTIVATION AND CARE TIPS.** They grow easily in full sun and average, well-drained soil, with plants set 18 in (45 cm) apart.

■ **PROPAGATION.** Division in spring every three years.

■ **PESTS AND DISEASES.** Occasionally rust or mildew in late summer; cut plants back to the ground.

Cerastium tomentosum

CENTRANTHUS
RED VALERIAN

RED VALERIAN (*Centranthus ruber*, sometimes listed as *Kentranthus ruber* or *Valeriana ruber*) grows readily, especially in cool-summer areas, and blooms for much of the summer. The large, showy heads of small red, pink or white fragrant flowers bloom again if the spent stems are cut back. They are excellent as cut flowers and attract butterflies. The bushy plants grow to 3 ft (90 cm) tall with blue- or grey-green leaves. Although not long-lived, red valerian is easily propagated and plants self-sow readily, except for the white-flowered type. It is effective grown towards the middle of a perennial border, along stone walls and in rock gardens.

■ **CULTIVATION AND CARE TIPS.** It grows in average, well-drained soil in full sun to partial shade. In poor soil, plants will be shorter than their usual 3 ft (90 cm); in poorly drained soil they will probably not survive the winter. Set plants 12–18 in (30–45 cm) apart. Hardy to −20°F (−28°C).

■ **PROPAGATION.** Division in spring every three or four years. Basal cuttings in early summer. Self-sow.

■ **PESTS AND DISEASES.** Seldom bothered.

Centranthus ruber

CERASTIUM
SNOW-IN-SUMMER

DENSE MATS OF DOWNY, silvery grey, fine-textured foliage and star-shaped pure white flowers make snow-in-summer (*Cerastium tomentosum*) a popular choice for planting in stone walls, in rock gardens, as an edging, or as a ground cover. Plants grow 6 in (15 cm) tall and spread 2 ft (60 cm), and can become invasive. The masses of ¾-in (18-mm) flowers cover the plants in early summer.

■ **SPECIES, VARIETIES AND CULTIVARS.** Several varieties are available, including 'Silver Carpet'. *C. biebersteinii* is less vigorous with not such grey leaves.

■ **CULTIVATION AND CARE TIPS.** It grows rampantly in full sun and poor to average garden soil; good drainage is essential. Shear plants lightly after flowering to prevent self-sowing. Set plants 12 in (30 cm) apart. Hardy to −40°F (−40°C).

■ **PROPAGATION.** Division in spring or fall. Softwood cuttings taken in summer after flowering. Seed.

■ **PESTS.** Seldom bothered, but foliage may become unattractive by autumn.

Chrysanthemum x morifolium

CHRYSANTHEMUM

CHRYSANTHEMUM, DAISY

SYNONYMOUS WITH AUTUMN, the garden, or florists' chrysanthemum (*C. × morifolium*) is a glorious addition to the garden in its innumerable shapes, colours and sizes. Plants grow 1–4 ft (30 cm–1.2 m) tall and can be rounded or tall and narrow in shape, usually with small grey-green leaves. The 1–6-in (2.5–15-cm) daisy-like flowers may be single, double or pompons, with some having special shapes described as button, spoon, quill or spider. All colours except blue have been developed. Depending on the size, chrysanthemums can be used singly, in groups, or massed in borders, beds and rock gardens, or used as an edging.

■ **SPECIES, VARIETIES AND CULTIVARS.** Pyrethrum, or painted daisy (*C. coccineum*) has 3-in (7.5-cm), single or double daisy-like pink, red, or white flowers with yellow centres on tall, single stems from early to midsummer. They are excellent as cut flowers. Growing 1–3 ft (30–90 cm) tall, the plants have ferny, dark green leaves and are best planted in groups of three.

Shasta daisy (*C. maximum*) has 3–5-in (7.5–12.5-cm) single or double flowers during the summer that are excellent for cutting. The long, narrow, shiny leaves and stems form 1–3 ft (30–90 cm) clumps. The long-blooming, daisy-like flowers of feverfew (*C. parthenium*, also called *Tanacetum parthenium* and *Matricaria parthenium*) are 1 in (2.5 cm) or less across and white or yellow, single or double, and superb for cutting. The plants can grow to 3 ft (90 cm) tall and sprawl unless sheared back when 12 in (30 cm) tall. Feverfew will readily self-sow.

■ **CULTIVATION AND CARE TIPS.** Plant chrysanthemums 12–18 in (30–45 cm) apart in full sun with humus-rich, well-drained soil. Double types of Shasta daisy do better in light shade. The chrysanthemums discussed here are generally hardy to −30°F (−34°C), but the garden chrysanthemums vary greatly in hardiness. Many gardeners choose to buy or start new plants each year. Garden chrysanthemums transplant easily, so that plants in bud or full bloom can be set into the garden in the autumn. If cuttings, seedlings, or divisions are set out in the spring, pinch out the growing tips of stems to six or eight leaves until mid-July; certain types, sometimes referred to as cushions, don't need pinching. Taller types must be staked. Deadhead regularly. Chrysanthemums benefit from a light summer mulch to keep soil moist and a winter mulch for protection.

■ **PROPAGATION.** Division of garden chrysanthemums in spring every year, pyrethrum every fourth year, and Shasta daisies every second or third year. Pyrethrum Shasta daisies and feverfew from seed. Cuttings taken in spring or summer.

■ **PESTS AND DISEASES.** Eelworm; leaf miners; capsid bugs; earwigs; red spider mites; aphids; slugs; snails; leaf spot; petal blight; mildew; root rot; rust; verticillium wilt; leafy gall.

Chrysanthemum parthenium 'ULTRA DOUBLE WHITE'

Chrysogonum virginianum 'MARK VIETTE'

CHRYSOGONUM

GOLDEN STAR, GREEN-AND-GOLD

GOLDEN STAR (*C. virginianum*) grows 4–6 in (10–15 cm) tall with small, pointed leaves and delicate, star-shaped 1½-in (4-cm) golden yellow flowers. In mild climates, the leaves are evergreen. Leaves vary from smooth to hairy and dark green to grey-green.

■ **CULTIVATION AND CARE TIPS.** Growing best in light to full shade, the plants bloom all summer, especially in cooler climates or if the soil remains evenly moist but well-drained. Spreading by seed or rooting stems, golden star makes a good ground cover, edging, or accent in a shaded wild flower or rock garden; it does not become invasive. Set plants 12 in (30 cm) apart in humus-rich, moist but well-drained soil. Hardy to −20°F (−29°C).

■ **PROPAGATION.** Division in spring or autumn.

■ **PESTS AND DISEASES.** Seldom bothered.

CIMICIFUGA

BLACK SNAKEROOT, BUGBANE

A GRACEFUL, DRAMATIC, low-maintenance plant for the back of a shady border, among shrubs, beside a pool or in open woodland, snakeroot produces large, open plants. Long, thin spires of white flowers arise in midsummer from the dark green, deeply cut and divided leaves. The seed spikes may be cut and dried for arrangements. Both may be used as fresh cut flowers as well.

■ **SPECIES, VARIETIES AND CULTIVARS.** Black snakeroot (*Cimicifuga racemosa*) grows to 6 ft (1.8 m) tall with creamy white flowers. The autumn-blooming Kamchatka bugbane (*C. simplex*) has arching, white flowers, more finely textured foliage and grows 2–4 ft (60 cm–1.20 m) tall.

■ **CULTIVATION AND CARE TIPS.** Long-lived once established, they bloom best in light shade but tolerate both full shade or sun. They must have deep, moist, humus-rich, well-drained soil. Flower spikes may need staking. Set plants 2 ft (60 cm) apart with the rhizome 1 in (2.5 cm) deep. Be patient for plants to grow for several years before blooming. Hardy to −40°F (−40°C).

■ **PROPAGATION.** Division in spring, only if more plants are needed. Sow seed outdoors as soon as ripened.

■ **PESTS AND DISEASES.** Seldom bothered.

Cimicifuga racemosa

CLEMATIS

Most often thought of as climbing plants, there are several shrubby perennial types that are easily grown and long-lived. Clematis are unusual in that the flowers have no actual petals but rather petal-like sepals. Most types have plumed seeds almost as showy as the flowers. Both flowers and seed heads may be used in arrangements.

■ **SPECIES, VARIETIES AND CULTIVARS.** Native to China, the tube clematis (*Clematis heracleifolia*) forms a mound 3 ft (90 cm) tall with coarse, broad, hairy leaves and spikes of fragrant blue flowers resembling hyacinths in late summer.

With sprawling growth, the solitary clematis (*C. integrifolia*) grows 2–4 ft (60 cm–1.2 m) tall with prominently veined leaves and 1-in (2.5-cm), bell-shaped lavender to violet-blue flowers in midsummer. A hybrid *C. × eriostemon* 'Hendersonii' is similar but with larger, indigo-blue flowers.

The ground clematis (*C. recta*) has slender twining stems growing 2–5 ft (60 cm–1.5 m) long and divided leaves. Plants are covered in masses of 1-in (2.5-cm) fragrant, star-shaped white flowers in early summer.

■ **CULTIVATION AND CARE TIPS.** Each of these clematis grows well in full sun to light shade and requires a humus-rich, moist but well-drained soil. A 2-in (5-cm) mulch of compost, or well-rotted manure, in summer will help to maintain the requisite cool soil. Care must be taken when cultivating around clematis as roots are easily damaged. Light staking is usually necessary, especially with ground clematis, or plants can be allowed to tumble over edges of raised beds, walls, or other plants. Trim back plants to 4–6 in (10–15 cm) tall in late autumn or early spring. Set plants 18 in (45 cm) apart. Hardy to −30°F (−34°C).

■ **PROPAGATION.** Division in spring. Cuttings in summer.

■ **PESTS AND DISEASES.** Slugs; aphids; earwigs; powdery mildew; clematis wilt; leaf spot. A virus disease causes yellow mottling of foliage and distortion of flowers.

Clematis integrifolia 'COERULA'

Coreopsis verticillata 'MOONBEAM'

COREOPSIS

TICKSEED

T HE SUNSHINE-YELLOW, daisy-like flowers of tickseed brighten borders and meadow gardens for much of the summer, especially if faded flowers are clipped off, or if the plants are cut back by one-third after the first flush of bloom. Very easily grown, the flowers are very long-lasting when cut.

■ **SPECIES, VARIETIES AND CULTIVARS.** The eared tickseed (*Coreopsis auriculata*) grows 1–2 ft (30–60 cm) tall with 1–2-in (2.5–5-cm) golden yellow flowers. The big-flowered tickseed (*C. grandiflora*) has narrow hairy leaves on 1–2 ft (30–60 cm) plants and 2–3-in (5–7.5-cm), long-stalked flowers, which are excellent for cutting. Very free-blooming and tolerant of dry soils, plants do not live long but readily self-sow. Lance tickseed (*C. lanceolata*) is similar, but it lives for a long time. Drought-tolerant and spreading slowly by under-

ground stems, threadleaf tickseed (*C. verticillata*) is another long-lived species. It grows 12–30 in (30–75 cm) tall with very thin, thread-like leaves and masses of 2-in (5-cm) flowers. The cultivars include 'Zagreb', a more compact form.

■ **CULTIVATION AND CARE TIPS.** The species needs full sun, but both threadleaf and eared tickseed can tolerate light shade. Soil need only be average, but must be well-drained. Set plants 12 in (30 cm) apart. Hardy to −30°F (−34°C).

■ **PROPAGATION.** Division in spring every three or four years except for *C. grandiflora*, which is usually started from seed each year. All types can be started from seed.

■ **PESTS AND DISEASES.** Froghoppers; slugs.

DELPHINIUM

LARKSPUR

CLASSIC PLANTS FOR the perennial border and one of the most spectacular but also one with pitfalls, larkspurs are known by their tall spikes of flowers, most often in shades of blue or purple. Plants grow 18 in–6 ft (45 cm–1.8 m) tall. They do best in cool, moist climates, but it is possible to grow them in other areas if expectations are lowered.

■ **SPECIES, VARIETIES AND CULTIVARS.** Many hybrid varieties of candle larkspur (*Delphinium elatum*) including doubles have been developed, growing to 6 ft (1.8 m). Each flower of these hybrids may be 1–3 in (2.5–7.5 cm) across, in shades of white, pink, lavender, blue, violet or purple. Remove all but three to five shoots in order to produce the largest stems and flowers.

The Chinese, or Siberian, larkspur (*D. grandiflorum*) is a short-lived perennial, often treated as an annual or biennial, but it flowers the first year from an early sowing. It grows 1–2 ft (30–60 cm) tall with finely divided leaves, and bears open spikes of blue, purple, or white funnel-shaped, long-spurred flowers.

Hybrid crosses of *D. elatum* and *D. grandiflorum* with some other species have yielded the popular 'Connecticut Yankee' strain, growing 24–30 in (60–75 cm) tall with bushy, branching plants as well as the 'Bellamosa' and 'Belladonna' hybrids, growing 3–4 ft (90 cm–1.2 m) tall with a long blooming season.

■ **CULTIVATION AND CARE TIPS.** They grow well in full sun to light shade and need a humus-rich, moist but well-drained, slightly alkaline soil. Mulching in the summer with several inches (centimetres) of compost or well-rotted manure keeps the roots cool and moist. Fertilize the plants in spring and again in early summer with a phosphorus- and potassium-rich mixture. Use long enough stakes to go 12 in (30 cm) into the ground and reach two-thirds of the flower stem; tie at 12-in (30-cm) intervals. If possible, choose a site protected from strong winds. Space shorter types 12–18 in (30–45 cm) apart and taller ones 24–30 in (60–75 cm) apart. Cut faded flowering stems off just below the flower cluster to encourage reblooming. Cut all stems back in autumn. Hardy to −40°F (−40°C).

Delphinium HYBRIDS

■ **PROPAGATION.** Division in spring every third or fourth year. Basal cuttings in spring. Sow seed in late summer outdoors as soon as ripened or store in sealed plastic bags in the refrigerator and sow in early spring indoors or late spring outdoors.

■ **PESTS AND DISEASES.** Slugs; snails; crown, root and stem rot; powdery mildew; mosaic; wilt; grey mould.

DIANTHUS

CARNATION, PINKS

THE DELICIOUS, SPICY fragrance of carnations and pinks have made them prized for centuries, both in the garden and as cut flowers. The blooms are usually in shades of pink, red, or white, sometimes with a contrasting eye, a single five-petalled flower, a semi-double, or a double with many petals, and with the petals fringed or toothed. Most types have attractive dark or grey-green, grass-like foliage that forms mounds or mats. They adapt readily to rock gardens, paths, and walls, and are excellent for edgings. Easily hybridized, there are numerous cultivars and much confusion as to proper naming.

■ **SPECIES, VARIETIES AND CULTIVARS.** The cottage pink, border carnation, or allwood pink (*Dianthus* × *allwoodii*) is a large, diverse group with many excellent varieties for the garden. The tufts of blue-green foliage grow 12 in (30 cm) tall and the flowers are like miniature carnations to 2 in (5 cm) across, single, semi-double, or double.

Wonderful for creating masses of colour, sweet william (*D. barbatus*) is best treated as a short-lived perennial or biennial, but it readily self-sows so plants remain in the garden for many years. Growing 12–18 in (30–45 cm) tall with dark green leaves, the sturdy stems bear flat or rounded clusters 3–6 in (7.5–15 cm) across of numerous ½–1-in (12 mm–2.5 cm) flowers, which are often varicoloured, but only lightly fragrant.

Dianthus deltoides 'ZING ROSE'

Dianthus plumarius

Maiden pink (*D. deltoides*) usually grows only 6 in (15 cm) tall, forming spreading mats of bright, semi-evergreen leaves. The early-summer, single flowers are less than 1 in (2.5 cm) across. Dainty Cheddar pink (*D. gratianopolitanus*) forms neat, tidy mats of blue-grey leaves 6 in (15 cm) tall. Blooming mainly in early summer, some flowering continues until autumn. The blooms are seldom more than ½-in (12 mm) across.

Cottage pink, wild pink or Scotch pink (*D. plumarius*) forms loose mounds or mats of grey-green leaves 12 in (30 cm) or so tall. The 1–2-in (2.5–5-cm) flowers may be single, semi-double or double and bloom over a long period.

The carnation (*D. caryophyllus*) is the flower purchased from florists. Although possible to grow in the garden, the other types of dianthus discussed are better suited.

■ **CULTIVATION, AND CARE TIPS.** Plants require full sun and do best in a sandy, humus-enriched well-drained, slightly alkaline soil. Poor drainage in winter is almost certain death, especially for low-growing types. They benefit from some loose winter protection, such as evergreen branches, in colder areas. They are best treated as biennials in hot climates. Set plants 8–12 in (20–30 cm) apart. Deadhead regularly to prolong blooming or prevent self-seeding. Hardy to −30°F (−34°C).

■ **PROPAGATION.** Seed. Cuttings in summer. Division in spring.

■ **PESTS AND DISEASES.** Aphids; thrips; leaf spot; mildew; rust; wilt; stem rot; grey mould.

Dicentra spectabilis

DICENTRA

BLEEDING HEART

ALL BLEEDING HEARTS are noted for their graceful shapes and unusually formed flowers, and are popular for cottage, rock and wild flower gardens. Most types are small-growing plants for the front of shaded beds or borders or a woodland garden, but one is taller and better suited to the middle of beds and borders. Bleeding hearts may self-sow but seldom become invasive.

■ **SPECIES, VARIETIES AND CULTIVARS.** Dutchman's breeches (*Dicentra cucullaria*) and squirrel corn (*D. canadensis*) are early spring-blooming wild flowers with white flowers. With both, the fern-like, 10–in (25-cm) foliage dies back after blooming.

Much better suited for a lightly shaded perennial border are the fringed bleeding heart (*D. eximia*) and the Pacific bleeding heart (*D. formosa*). These form neat mounds 1 ft (30 cm) tall, with grey-green, feathery foliage and sprays of rose-pink, heart-shaped flowers from early spring until frost. The two species are difficult to distinguish. Hybrids and cultivars of both species are available, including 'Bountiful' and 'Adrian Bloom'. These are more tolerant of direct sun and have flowers in various shades of pink and red.

Common bleeding heart (*D. spectabilis*) forms a loose, open plant 2–3 ft (60–90 cm) tall, with divided leaves. In late spring, arching sprays of 1½-in (4-cm), rose-pink, heart-shaped flowers emerge. A pure white form is also available. Plants die back by midsummer, so they must be surrounded by other plants.

■ **CULTIVATION AND CARE TIPS.** They grow best with light to full shade in humus-rich, moist but well-drained soil. A summer mulch of compost or well-rotted manure will keep the soil cool and moist. Space the small-growing types 12 in (30 cm) apart and common bleeding heart 2 ft (60 cm) apart. Deadhead regularly to prolong blooming. Hardy to −40°F (−40°C).

■ **PROPAGATION.** Division in spring immediately after blooming, every three or four years. Seed. Root cuttings.

■ **PESTS AND DISEASES.** Seldom bothered.

Dictamnus alba 'PURPUREA'

DICTAMNUS
BURNING BUSH

A VERY LONG-LIVED, low-maintenance perennial, burning bush (*D. alba*, also called *D. fraxinella*) grows to a shrubby 2–3 ft (60–90 cm) tall with glossy, dark green leaves that remain attractive until frost. If a match is held to the flowers or seeds on a still summer evening, the volatile oils given off by the plant will set off a flash of light – hence the common name. When crushed, the flowers and the foliage have the scent of lemons. Produced in numerous long spikes in early summer, the 1–2-in (2.5–5-cm) white blooms are good for cutting and are followed by interesting star-shaped seed pods useful in dried arrangements. Touching the flowers and seeds may cause an allergic reaction.

■ **CULTIVATION AND CARE TIPS.** It has deep roots, so does not transplant well and needs several years to become established, at which time it tolerates drought. Grow in full sun or very light shade with humus-rich, moist but well-drained soil. Set plants 3 ft (90 cm) apart. Hardy to −40°F (−40°C).

■ **PROPAGATION.** Seed sown outdoors in the fall sprout the following spring; seeds saved until the spring will germinate more readily if boiling water is poured over them. It may be three or four years before new plants bloom.

■ **PESTS AND DISEASES.** Seldom bothered.

DIGITALIS
FOXGLOVE

FOXGLOVE'S TALL SPIRES of velvety, dotted bells rising from low clumps of leaves provide a dramatic statement in the early summer garden. Use as a vertical accent in the middle to the back of a border, or let plants naturalize in an informal garden.

■ **SPECIES, VARIETIES AND CULTIVARS.** Common foxglove (*Digitalis purpurea*) is a biennial growing 4 ft (1.2 m) or taller with 2-in (5-cm) flowers in white or shades of pink or purple; plants readily self-sow. The Merton hybrid foxgloves (*D. × mertonensis*) are perennials with pink, rose, or red flowers on spikes growing to 3 ft (90 cm) tall. The yellow foxglove (*D. grandiflora*, or *D. ambigua*) is a perennial with 2–3-in (5–7.5-cm) creamy yellow flowers dotted with brown on 3-ft (90-cm) stems. The straw foxglove (*D. lutea*) has white to pale yellow flowers on 1–2-ft (30–60-cm) spikes.

■ **CULTIVATION AND CARE TIPS.** They grow best in a humus-rich, moist but well-drained soil and full sun or partial shade. Remove faded flower stems if self-sowing is not desired; this may also encourage re-blooming. Set plants 12–18 in (30–45 cm) apart. Hardy to −30°F (−34°C). A winter mulch of evergreen branches is helpful where there is little snow cover.

■ **PROPAGATION.** Division in spring after blooming. Seed sown outdoors in late summer for flowers the following year.

■ **PESTS AND DISEASES.** Crown and root rot may develop if the ground is over-wet in winter.

Digitalis purpurea

Doronicum caucasicum

DORONICUM
LEOPARD'S BANE

GROWING 12–18 IN (30–45 cm) tall, the tidy, spreading mounds of glossy green, heart-shaped leaves make leopard's bane (*Doronicum caucasicum*, also called *D. cordatum*) a good plant for the front of a border, a rock garden, or planted among spring bulbs and shrubs. In late spring or early summer the plants are covered with yellow, daisy-like 2-in (5-cm) flowers. They are long-lasting when cut but close at night. Leopard's bane goes dormant by late summer, so combine it with other plants that will fill in around it. The variety 'Miss Mason' has foliage that stays attractive until frost.

■ **CULTIVATION AND CARE TIPS.** They need humus-rich, moist but well-drained soil and either full sun or light shade. Set plants 12 in (30 cm) apart. Hardy to −30°F (−34°C).

■ **PROPAGATION.** Division every four years, in very early spring or late summer. Seed.

■ **PESTS AND DISEASES.** Powdery mildew.

ECHINACEA
PURPLE CONE FLOWER

THIS LOW-MAINTENANCE, summer-blooming wild flower is excellent when massed in informal plantings, or as a bold specimen in the middle or back of a border. Growing 2–4 ft (60 cm–1.2 m) tall, purple cone flowers have coarse, hairy stems and leaves and long-stalked, 4–6-in (10–15-cm) daisy-like flowers that bloom over a long period. The cone part, or centre, of the flower is a brownish-orange and the rays, or petals, are magenta-pink and drooping. There are also white forms, plus other cultivars of various colours. The flowers attract butterflies, the blooms are good for cutting and the dried cones add texture to dried arrangements.

■ **CULTIVATION AND CARE TIPS.** Long-lived, the plants tolerate drought and grow well in a humus-rich, sandy soil that is well-drained; they tolerate either full sun or light shade. Staking is unnecessary except in very rich soil. Deadhead regularly to prolong blooming. Plant 18 in (45 cm) apart. Hardy to −40°F (−40°C).

■ **PROPAGATION.** Division every four years in early spring. Seed, but plants are variable.

■ **PESTS AND DISEASES.** Seldom bothered.

Echinacea purpurea

Echinops ritro

ECHINOPS

GLOBE THISTLE

AN UNUSUAL, EYE-CATCHING addition to the middle or back of flower beds or borders, as a specimen among shrubs, or in a meadow garden, globe thistles are also popular because they are good for arrangements, either fresh or dried. If drying, cut just before they open and hang upside down. The 1–2-in (2.5–5-cm) globe-like clusters of tiny, steel-blue flowers are borne on branching stems. Blooming for several months during summer, the flowers attract bees by day and moths at night. There is much confusion as to the scientific naming of this plant but most are sold as *Echinops ritro* or *E. humilis*. 'Taplow Blue' is a recommended variety. Plants grow 3–5 ft (90 cm–1.5 m) tall, with dark-green thistle-like leaves with a downy white underside.

■ **CULTIVATION AND CARE TIPS.** They are easily grown in full sun and almost any soil and tolerate heat and drought once established because of deep roots. Staking may be required if soil is rich. Set plants 18–24 in (45–60 cm) apart. Hardy to −30°F (−34°C).

■ **PROPAGATION.** Division in early spring, if necessary. Root cuttings. Seed, but plants are variable.

■ **PESTS AND DISEASES.** Seldom bothered.

ERIGERON

FLEABANE

RESEMBLING ASTERS, with 2-in (5-cm) delicate, daisy-like flowers in shades of blue, pink, or white with yellow centres, fleabanes bloom during early and mid-summer. The flowers are excellent for cutting.

■ **SPECIES, VARIETIES AND CULTIVARS.** A low-maintenance plant, the best fleabanes are the various hybrids, including lavender 'Quakeress', bright pink 'Gaiety', and pale pink 'Felicity'. Plants are bushy and 18–30 in (45–75 cm) tall with shiny green leaves. Short types can be used in the rock garden. In the perennial garden, they are best when planted in groups of at least three; or allow to naturalize in a meadow garden, as plants readily self-sow.

■ **CULTIVATION AND CARE TIPS.** They do best in sandy, well-drained soil, and full sun in regions with cool summers but will withstand hotter temperatures with light shade. Set plants 12–18 in (30–45 cm) apart. Deadhead regularly to prolong blooming. Hardy to −10°F (−23°C).

■ **PROPAGATION.** Division or basal cuttings in early spring. Seed.

■ **PESTS AND DISEASES.** Seldom bothered.

Erigeron

Eryngium HYBRID

ERYNGIUM

SEA HOLLY

A STRIKING, THISTLE-LIKE plant growing 2–4 ft (60 cm–1.2 m) tall, sea holly has prickly blue-grey foliage and white or purplish, 1-in (2.5-cm) cone-shaped flowers surrounded by a ruff of leaves. These branching stems of summer-blooming flowers are excellent for fresh or dried arrangements. Use the plants as an accent in the middle of flower beds and borders, in a rock garden, or a naturalized meadow garden.

■ **SPECIES, VARIETIES AND CULTIVARS.** There is much disagreement over the identification of sea hollies, and discrepancy among what plants are actually being sold.

Amethyst sea holly (*Eryngium amethystinum*) grows 2 ft (60 cm) tall with white-veined leaves and blue-purple flowers; it is hardy to −40°F (−40°C). Flat-leaved sea holly (*E. planum*) grows 3 ft (90 cm) tall and has small blue flowers. True sea holly (*E. maritimum*) grows 12 in (30 cm) tall with white or pale blue flowers. Zabel's sea holly (*E. × zabelii*) grows 24–30 in (60–75

cm) tall with blue flowers. Alpine sea holly (*E. alpinum*) grows 2 ft (60 cm) tall; the flowers have a feathery blue ruff. The last two species are tolerant of clay soils and light shade. Giant sea holly (*E. giganteum*) is a biennial that grows 2–3 ft (60–90 cm) tall with greenish-white flowers. Mediterranean sea holly (*E. bourgatii*) grows 2 ft (60 cm) tall with white-veined leaves and slender white flower ruffs.

■ **CULTIVATION AND CARE TIPS.** They need sandy, well-drained soil and full sun. Long-lived, once planted they should not be disturbed. Deadhead to prevent self-sowing, unless desired. Set plants 12–24 in (30–60 cm) apart. Hardy to −20°F (−28°C).

■ **PROPAGATION.** Root cuttings, taken in spring only if absolutely necessary. Seed sown as soon as ripe will germinate the following spring; young plants transplant easily.

■ **PESTS AND DISEASES.** Seldom bothered.

Eupatorium purpureum

EUPATORIUM

MIST FLOWER, JOE-PYE WEED

BILLOWY CLUSTERS OF tiny flowers in shades of blue or pink during late summer and autumn make these plants attractive in flower beds or borders and meadow gardens. Joe-Pye weed is especially effective naturalized in the damp soil beside streams and around marshes. Both mist flower and Joe-Pye weed attract butterflies and make good cut flowers.

■ **SPECIES, VARIETIES AND CULTIVARS.** Mist flower, or hardy ageratum, (*Eupatorium coelestinum*) resembles the annual ageratum with its fluffy flower-heads of lavender-blue on 2-ft (60-cm) plants. The wrinkled leaves are thin and coarsely toothed. In sandy soil, plants may become invasive.

There are several species of eupatorium called Joe-Pye weed, including hollow Joe-Pye weed (*E. fistulosum*), hollow stems growing 6 ft (1.8 m) tall with rounded clusters of mauve flowers; spotted Joe-Pye weed (*E. maculatum*), speckled stems growing to 10 ft (3 m) with loose, open clusters of purple flowers; and common Joe-Pye weed or gravel root (*E. purpureum*), growing 6 ft (1.8 m) tall with large clusters of rose pink to purplish flowers.

■ **CULTIVATION AND CARE TIPS.** Both mist flower and Joe-Pye weed grow easily in full sun and a wide range of average to moist soils. Light shade is tolerated but plants bloom less. Set mist flower 18 in (45 cm) apart and Joe-Pye weed 3 ft (90 cm) apart. Mist flower is hardy to −20°F (−28°C) and Joe-Pye weed to −40°F (−40°C).

■ **PROPAGATION.** Division in spring, cuttings in summer, or seed. Mist flower needs dividing every two or three years.

■ **PESTS AND DISEASES.** Seldom bothered.

EUPHORBIA

SPURGE

ALTHOUGH THERE ARE over 1600 different spurges, only a few are of horticultural interest. Spurges are characterized by showy bracts, with very tiny flowers in the centre. They have a milky sap, which can be a skin irritant.

■ **SPECIES, VARIETIES AND CULTIVARS.** Cushion spurge (*Euphorbia epithymoides*, also called *E. polychroma*) forms an evenly rounded mound 12 in (30 cm) tall and 2 ft (60 cm) wide. The spring-blooming bracts are golden yellow, 1-in (2.5-cm) wide, and leaves turn rose-coloured in the autumn. It may not do well in hot, humid climates.

E. griffithii 'Fireglow' grows to 3 ft (90 cm) tall. The leaves have a pale pink midrib and the red bracts are in 2–4-in (5–10-cm) clusters during early summer. Because it easily tolerates dry soil, myrtle spurge (*E. myrsinites*) is a good choice for a rock garden or in a stone wall. A low, trailing plant, it is mainly grown for its blue-green leaves that remain on the plant year-round. The flowers are bright yellow in spring.

Resembling baby's breath, flowering spurge (*E. corollata*) grows 2 ft (60 cm) tall with loose clusters of tiny, showy white bracts in summer and are excellent for cutting. Sear cut stems in a candle flame to seal the end. Foliage turns red in the autumn.

■ **CULTIVATION AND CARE TIPS.** Long-lived, these spurges grow best in full sun in dry, sandy soil. Light shade is beneficial in hot areas. Plants readily self-sow. Set plants 12–18 in (30–45 cm) apart. Hardy to −20°F (−28°C).

■ **PROPAGATION.** They do not transplant well, but if necessary, division in early spring. Seed. Cuttings.

■ **PESTS AND DISEASES.** Grey mould.

Euphorbia epithymoides

Athyrium filix-femina

FERNS

IMAGINE A LUSH, fern-filled glade on a hot summer's day and the usefulness of ferns in the garden is readily apparent. They are at their best when massed, especially under trees, along a wall, surrounding a pool, or on the north side of a house. They are very effective when combined with the early spring-flowering bulbs. The leaf form of a fern is called a frond, and ferns are reproduced by spores rather than seeds. The fronds are superb as foliage in flower arrangements.

■ **SPECIES, VARIETIES AND CULTIVARS.** Considered one of the most beautiful ferns, maidenhair fern (*Adiantum pedatum*) has bright green, lacy fronds and black stems 12–18 in (30–45 cm) tall. Spreading slowly by rhizomes, it requires humus-rich, moist but well-drained soil and shade.

The lady fern (*Athyrium filix-femina*) grows in crowns with lacy fronds 2–3 ft (60–90 cm) tall. It tolerates a wide range of soils and grows in both sun or shade.

For drama in large areas, the ostrich feather fern (*Matteuccia pensylvanica*) with bright green, 4–6-ft (1.2–1.8-m) fronds is an effective ground cover. Spreading by rhizomes, it grows well in light shade and average soil or full sun if the soil is kept moist.

Sensitive fern (*Onoclea sensibilis*) has unusual grey-green fronds growing 2 ft (60 cm) tall and stalks with spore-bearing 'pods' prized for flower arrangements. It readily spreads by rhizomes in sun or shade and moist garden soil.

The cinnamon fern (*Osmunda cinnamomea*) grows 4–6 ft (1.2–1.8 m) tall with pale green fronds turning golden, then brown in the autumn. Tolerating average garden soil, this crown-spreading fern grows the biggest in moist soil in full sun or light shade.

The royal fern (*Osmunda regalis*) grows 4–6 ft (1.2–1.8 m) tall with dramatic fronds that are unusual in that there are fertile flower-like spikes at the tips of some. Constantly moist, acidic soil and shade are necessary. Plants spread slowly from crowns.

The dainty evergreen common polypody (*Polypodium virginianum*) spreads by rhizomes over rocks and fallen trees with 6–10-in (15–25-cm) leathery fronds. A wide range of conditions is tolerated but best growth is with moist but well-drained soil and light shade.

Related to the Boston fern, the evergreen Christmas fern (*Polystichum acrostichoides*) is one of the easiest ferns to grow. Tolerant of a wide range of conditions, light shade and humus-rich, moist but well-drained soil is ideal. It spreads slowly by rhizomes.

■ **CULTIVATION AND CARE TIPS.** In general, they grow best in a shady location with humus-rich, loose soil that is moist but well-drained and a light mulch of compost, bark, or shredded leaves. Set plants 12–30 in (30–75 cm) apart. Hardy to −40°F (−40°C).

■ **PROPAGATION.** Division of creeping types at any time and ones with crowns when dormant in early spring or late autumn.

■ **PESTS AND DISEASES.** Some ferns may be bothered by slugs, snails and rust.

Osmunda cinnamomea

Filipendula vulgaris 'FLORE-PLENO'

FILIPENDULA

QUEEN-OF-THE-PRAIRIE, MEADOW SWEET, DROPWORT

THE PLUMY CLUSTERS OF tiny pink or white flowers and the lush, dark green, compound leaves of these plants make them a source of fine texture in the garden. The flowers are good for cutting, if picked before they are fully open.

■ **SPECIES, VARIETIES AND CULTIVARS.** Queen-of-the-prairie (*F. rubra*) sends up numerous stalks 4–7 ft (1.2–2.1 m) tall with clusters of rosy pink, fragrant flowers at the tips in mid-summer. Meadow sweet (*F. ulmaria*) has fragrant, white flower clusters in early summer on 3–5-ft (90-cm–1.5-m) plants. Use these two plants in the back of a border, planted among shrubs, or beside a stream. Dropwort (*F. vulgaris*, also called *F. hexapetala*) has fern-like leaves in a ground-hugging clump and ivory flowers on 18–24-in (45–60 cm) stalks in early summer; it readily self-sows. Plant at the front of a border or in a woodland garden.

■ **CULTIVATION AND CARE TIPS.** Provide a humus-rich, moist but well-drained soil; dropwort tolerates some dryness. Plants do best in light shade, but grow in full sun in cooler, northern climates. Set meadow sweet and queen-of-the-prairie 2 ft (60 cm) apart and dropwort 12 in (30 cm) apart. Hardy to −40°F (−40°C). If there is no snow cover in cold areas, mulch with leaves to protect the roots.

■ **PROPAGATION.** Division in spring. Seed.

■ **PESTS AND DISEASES.** Powdery mildew, if plants are grown in soil too dry.

Galium odoratum

GALIUM

GAILLARDIA

BLANKET FLOWER

BLANKET FLOWERS READILY PRODUCE brightly coloured, daisy-like 3–4-in (7.5–10-cm) blooms for much of the summer. The flowers are various combinations of yellow, gold and red, often with purple centres. The taller-growing types are good for cutting.

■ **SPECIES, VARIETIES AND CULTIVARS.** The common perennial blanket flower (*G. aristata*) is a sprawling 2–3-ft (60–90-cm) plant with grey-green, hairy leaves. Excellent for the meadow or wild garden, it is one of the main parents of many popular hybrids, including 'Burgundy', 'Dazzler', and 'Goblin'.

■ **CULTIVATION AND CARE TIPS.** They tend to be short-lived in fertile, moist soils, but last longer with full sun in average to poor, very well-drained soil, especially in winter. Deadhead and trim back plants in late summer for more bloom in the autumn. If plants do not bloom, divide them in early spring. Set plants 6–18 in (15–45 cm) apart. Hardy to −40°F (−40°C).

■ **PROPAGATION.** Division in early spring. Basal cuttings in late summer or root cuttings in autumn and overwintered in a coldframe. Seed.

■ **PESTS AND DISEASES.** Downy mildew.

Gaillardia HYBRID

GALIUM

SWEET WOODRUFF

A LOW-MAINTENANCE ground cover for shaded areas, sweet woodruff (*Galium odoratum*, also known as *Asperula odorata*) is used fresh as an herb. The dried leaves are used to flavour liqueurs and scent insect-repelling sachets. Small, star-shaped fragrant white flowers are scattered across the tops of the 6–8-in (15–20-cm) mounds of thin, whorled leaves in spring and early summer.

■ **CULTIVATION AND CARE TIPS.** It prefers partial shade in moist but well-drained, humus-rich soil. Plant 12 in (30 cm) apart. Hardy to −30°F (−34°C).

■ **PROPAGATION.** Division in spring or autumn, as desired, although seldom required.

■ **PESTS AND DISEASES.** Seldom bothered.

GERANIUM

CRANE'S-BILL

TRUE GERANIUMS, not the summer bedding plants that are the genus *Pelargonium*, are lovely perennials with delicate 1–2-in (2.5–5-cm) pastel flowers often borne all summer long. There are many different species for the garden, with most growing as compact or open mounds. The attractive foliage is rounded and usually finely divided and toothed. They are best used towards the front of a border or along paths.

■ **SPECIES, VARIETIES AND CULTIVARS.** *Geranium × cantabrigiense* forms a 6–12-in (15–30-cm), slowly spreading mat of scented green leaves. Bright rose-pink flowers bloom in late spring and occasionally through the summer.

G. endressii 'Wargrave Pink' grows 2 ft (60 cm) tall and spreads to 3 ft (90 cm). The warm-pink, 1½-in (4-cm) flowers are borne throughout summer in cool climates and for a shorter period in hotter areas unless soil is kept evenly moist.

The lilac crane's-bill is *G. himalayense*, but it may also be listed as *G. grandiflorum* or *G. meeboldii*. Spreading mounds combine with 2-in (5-cm) blue flowers with purple veins. Big-root crane's-bill (*G. macrorrhizum*) makes an aromatic ground cover growing 12–18 in (30–45 cm) tall. In late spring and early summer, plants produce dense clusters of 1-in (2.5-cm) pink, magenta, or white flowers.

G. maculatum has loose, open growth to 2 ft (60 cm) tall and pink flowers in spring. It is good for lightly shaded wild flower gardens. *G. × oxonianum* 'Claridge Druce' forms a broad mound 2 ft (60 cm) tall with gray-green leaves and 2-in (5-cm) trumpet-shaped pink flowers with darker veins.

Blood-red crane's-bill (*G. sanguineum*) forms a mound 12–18 in (30–45 cm) tall with long-blooming, 1-in (2.5-cm), pink to magenta flowers. It is highly adaptable to various climates and also self-sows readily. If soil is too rich, it will spread excessively. Foliage turns deep red in autumn.

Two species are very good for the rock garden, *G. cinereum* and *G. dalmaticum*. Both grow 4–6 in (10–15 cm) tall, with lilac, magenta, pink or white flowers.

■ **CULTIVATION AND CARE TIPS.** They bloom best in full sun, but in hotter climates plants grow better with light shade. Average, moist but well-drained soil is best; overly rich soil encourages rampant growth. Set plants 12 in (30 cm) apart. Hardy to −30°F (−34°C).

■ **PROPAGATION.** Division in spring every four years or when clumps begin to deteriorate. Seed for species. Cuttings in summer.

■ **PESTS AND DISEASES.** Slugs. Rust is more prevalent on wild geranium species.

Geranium 'JOHNSON'S BLUE'

Geum 'MRS BRADSHAW'

GEUM

GEUM, AVENS

GEUMS FORM LOW CLUMPS of dark green leaves with thin, branching stems bearing 1½-in (4-cm) red, yellow, or orange flowers with wavy petals during summer. Lower-growing types are good in rock gardens; the taller ones (good for cutting) are best used toward the front of beds and borders.

■ **SPECIES, VARIETIES AND CULTIVARS.** *Geum rivale* 'Leonard' grows 12 in (30 cm) tall and has copper-rose, bell-shaped flowers on red stems. It must have moist soil and light shade. Hardy to −40°F (−40°C). There are a number of hybrid cultivars of the taller type, and most grow 18–24 in (45–60 cm) tall.

■ **CULTIVATION AND CARE TIPS.** They grow best in full sun in cool-summer areas, but light shade is preferable in hot climates. Soil must be humus-rich and moist but well-drained. Soggy soil in winter is fatal. Plants are slow to become established, and the varieties listed will not need dividing for many years. Set plants 12–18 in (30–45 cm) apart; they are best in groups of three. Deadhead regularly to prolong blooming. The taller hybrids are hardy to −20°F (−28°C) with a loose winter mulch.

■ **PROPAGATION.** Division in spring or late summer.

■ **PESTS AND DISEASES.** Seldom bothered.

BABY'S BREATH

THE BILLOWING CLOUDS of tiny white or pink flowers of baby's breath provide a fine-textured addition to the flower garden as well as to both fresh and dried bouquets. The thin, wiry, branching stems have a few narrow, grey-green leaves.

■ **SPECIES, VARIETIES, AND CULTIVARS.** Long-lived *G. paniculata* grows 18–36 in (45–90 cm) tall, depending on the variety, from thick, fleshy taproots that do not transplant well. The sprays of ¼-in (6-mm) flowers are produced during summer. Plants may become top-heavy and should be staked early in the season. With a long growing season, a second bloom is possible by trimming plants back after the first one. Hybrid cultivars include 'Bristol Fairy' and 'Pink Star'. Creeping baby's breath (*G. reptans*) grows 4–12 in (10–30 cm) tall with masses of whitish-pink flowers. This is best in rock gardens or spilling over walls.

■ **CULTIVATION AND CARE TIPS.** It grows in full sun with average, well-drained, alkaline soil. Plant 1–2 ft (30–60 cm) apart, in early spring. Many named varieties are grafted; set the graft union 1–2 in (2.5–5 cm) below the soil. Hardy to −30°F (−34°C), applying a loose mulch in winter after the ground is frozen.

■ **PROPAGATION.** The best kinds are purchased as grafted plants. Ordinary forms are grown from seeds or cuttings.

■ **PESTS AND DISEASES.** Seldom bothered.

Gypsophila paniculata 'COMPACTA-PLENA'

Helenium hoopesii

HELENIUM
SNEEZEWEED

LARGE PLANTS FOR THE middle to back of informal borders, in meadows or planted among shrubs, sneezeweed provides bright colours in the summer and fall. Daisy-like flowers with drooping yellow, orange or mahogany petals and prominent dark centres are borne profusely in branching clusters. The flowers are good for cutting, and plants are long-lived and never invasive.

■ **SPECIES, VARIETIES AND CULTIVARS.** Common sneezeweed, or Helen flower (*H. autumnale*) grows 6 feet (1.8 m) tall with each flower 2 in (5 cm) wide. Orange sneezeweed (*H. hoopesii*) grows 2 ft (60 cm) tall and blooms in early summer with large yellow-orange or gold flowers. It tolerates light shade.

■ **CULTIVATION AND CARE TIPS.** It grows well in full sun with a moist but well-drained, humus-rich soil, but tolerates a range of soils. Pinch out growing tips of taller-growing types in spring to make plants shorter and bushier. Provide staking for support. Set 18–24 in (45–60 cm) apart. Hardy to −40°F (−40°C).

■ **PROPAGATION.** Division in spring every two or three years. Cuttings. Species from seed.

■ **PESTS AND DISEASES.** Slugs; tortrix caterpillars. A virus disease turns the flowers green.

HELIOPSIS
FALSE SUNFLOWER

VIGOROUS, BOLD PLANTS with dark green foliage, false sunflowers have abundant clusters of golden, daisy-like flowers 2–4 in (5–10 cm) across, with slightly darker centres, blooming from summer through autumn. The species is best planted in an area where it can naturalize by self-sowing. Hybrid cultivars are also good at the back of flower borders, the centre of beds, or among shrubs. Cut flowers are long-lasting.

Heliopsis helianthoides varies in the wild, but is generally 5 ft (1.5 m) tall. Hybrids are usually shorter, growing 2–3 ft (60–90 cm) tall. 'Golden Plume' has double deep-yellow flowers.

■ **CULTIVATION AND CARE TIPS.** Although drought-tolerant, they grow best in full sun with average to humus-rich, moist but well-drained soil. Deadhead regularly to prolong blooming. Set plants 2 ft (60 cm) apart. Hardy to −30°F (−34°C).

■ **PROPAGATION.** Division in early spring every three or four years. Seed in spring or summer.

■ **PESTS AND DISEASES.** Seldom bothered.

Heliopsis helianthoides

Helleborus orientalis

HELLEBORUS

HELLEBORE

ALTHOUGH NOT ALWAYS as early-blooming as advertised, hellebores are still among the earliest perennials to flower, with blooming time varying from midwinter to spring, depending on the climate. Lasting a month or more, the nodding flowers are able to withstand cold temperatures and snow. Totally unrelated to roses, the flowers have five petal-like sepals and prominent golden stamens in the centre. Hellebores have long-stemmed, segmented leaves growing 12–18 in (30–45 cm) tall and may self-sow but are never invasive. Choose a site where they can be enjoyed at close range, such as near a doorway. They are good for cutting, if stem ends are seared in a flame immediately. Plants may cause an allergic reaction in some people.

■ **SPECIES, VARIETIES AND CULTIVARS.** Christmas rose (*Helleborus niger*) grows 12 in (30 cm) tall with 2–4-in (5–10 cm) white flowers tinged with pink or green, blooming from midwinter to early spring, one to three to a stem. Foliage is thick, evergreen, and saw-toothed. Hardy to −40°F (−40°C). Lenten rose (*H. orientalis*) blooms from late winter through spring with 2-in (5-cm) flowers that may be cream, purple-pink, maroon-brown, or greenish-white, sometimes with rose-purple spots. This 18-in (45 cm) tall species hybridizes readily and there are many forms, all of which are among the easiest to grow of the hellebores. Hardy to −30°F (−34°C).

Corsican hellebore (*H. argutifolius*, also listed as *H. corsicus* or *H. lividus corsicus*) has large clusters of pale green 1-in (2.5-cm) flowers in early spring on leafy stems 1–2 ft (30–60 cm) tall. Hardy to −20°F (−28°C). Stinking hellebore (*H. foetidus*) has clusters of pale green 1-in (2.5-cm) flowers, rimmed in purple as they age, on leafy stems 12–18 in (30–45 cm) tall. Hardy to −40°F (−40°C).

■ **CULTIVATION AND CARE TIPS.** Ideally, they need sun in the winter and shade in the summer with a humus-rich, neutral, moist but well-drained soil. Planting under deciduous trees or among other perennials are ways of achieving this. Do not allow soil to dry out in summer; a mulch is beneficial. Set plants 18 in (45 cm) apart with the crown 1 in (2.5 cm) below the soil line and allow several years for the long-lived plants to become established before they bloom well. Winter protection of various types may be used, including mulching loosely with oak leaves, covering with pine branches or building a plastic-covered frame to set over plants.

■ **PROPAGATION.** Division of the roots in spring after flowering or in autumn is possible but not recommended. Seed sown as soon as ripened.

■ **PESTS AND DISEASES.** Leaf spot.

Helleborus argutifolius

Hemerocallis 'STELLA D'OR'

HEMEROCALLIS

Day Lily

Easily grown and widely adaptable, day lilies have become among the most popular of all perennial plants, with thousands of different hybrid varieties. For a long period during summer, leafless stalks rise from the thick clumps of arching, grassy leaves änd bear open clusters of lily-like, sometimes fragrant, flowers. Each flower lasts only a day, but a plant may produce dozens during a season.

Depending on the height, day lilies may be used at the front, middle, back or centre of flower beds and borders. Smaller types are particularly good in rock gardens. Day lilies are also quite effective used as an edging, grown among shrubs, or massed in an informal or naturalistic setting.

■ **SPECIES, VARIETIES AND CULTIVARS.** The original species have yellow or orange flowers, but the colours of the hybrid cultivars are extremely varied, often with a contrasting stripe, edge or throat. Most have six petals, but some are doubles, and petals may be frilled or ruffled. The size of the plants in bloom varies from 12 in (30 cm) to over 6 ft (1.8 m) and flower size from 2–8 in (5–20 cm) across. Depending on the cultivar, bloom time can be late spring, summer, or autumn, and some types bloom repeatedly.

■ **CULTIVATION AND CARE TIPS.** They thrive in sun or light shade. Although a wide range of soil is tolerated, best growth is with a humus-rich, moist but well-drained soil. Extra watering during hot weather is recommended, but too much fertilizer will force plants into excessive growth at the cost of bloom. Specimen plants should be deadheaded; this is impossible with massed plantings. Set shorter types 12–18 in (30–45 cm) apart and larger ones 2 ft (60 cm) apart. Types that go dormant are hardy to −30°F (−34°C); evergreen and semi-evergreen types vary in hardiness and are best in warmer climates.

■ **PROPAGATION.** Division of clumps of rhizomatous roots in late summer or autumn, with clumps usually becoming overcrowded after about four to six years. Plantlets that develop on flower stalks can be removed and rooted.

■ **PESTS AND DISEASES.** Seldom bothered.

SWEET ROCKET, DAMASK VIOLET

SWEET ROCKET (*Hesperis matronalis*) is a lovely, cottage garden plant, resembling phlox, with wonderfully fragrant elongated clusters of lavender, purple, mauve or white ½-in (12-mm) flowers from late spring to midsummer. Good for cut flowers, sweet rocket is short-lived as a perennial, but self-sows readily. The bushy plants grow 2–3 ft (60–90 cm) tall and can be used in the flower border or in meadow gardens. 'Candidissima' is a dwarf white cultivar.

■ **CULTIVATION AND CARE TIPS.** It thrives best in full sun or partial shade with moist but well-drained alkaline soil. Set plants 18 in (45 cm) apart. Deadhead regularly to prolong blooming. Hardy to −40°F (−40°C).

■ **PROPAGATION.** Seeds

■ **PESTS AND DISEASES.** Seldom bothered.

Hesperis matronalis

Heuchera sanguinea 'CHATTERBOX'

CORAL BELLS

CORAL BELLS (*Heuchera sanguinea*) give a light, airy touch when planted in a rock garden, at the front of a flower bed, among shrubs, or as an edging to a path. From late spring through summer, wiry stems of tiny pink, red, or white bell-shaped flowers emerge from the low-growing clumps of rounded, mottled leaves that are evergreen in mild climates. The long-lasting flowers are good for cutting. The clumps grow 6–10 in (15–25 cm) tall and the flower stalks 1–2 ft (30–60 cm) tall. There are a number of excellent hybrid cultivars available, including 'Bressingham Blaze', 'Pearl Drops' and 'Scintillation'.

■ **CULTIVATION AND CARE TIPS.** They grow best with a humus-rich, moist but well-drained soil. Good drainage in winter is essential. Choose a site with full sun or light shade, with the latter preferable in hot, dry climates. Space plants 12 in (30 cm) apart and set crowns 1 in (2.5 cm) deep in spring. Deadhead regularly to prolong blooming. Hardy to −40°F (−40°C). Mulch with evergreen branches after the ground has frozen to prevent winter heaving of roots.

■ **PROPAGATION.** Division in spring or autumn, usually every three to five years, or when the crown becomes woody. Younger plants can be divided for increase.

■ **PESTS AND DISEASES.** Leafy gall.

Hibiscus moscheutos HYBRID

HIBISCUS

ROSE MALLOW, HIBISCUS

EXOTIC AND BOLD, rose mallow (*Hibiscus moscheutos*) makes a dramatic statement in the garden with the 6–12-in (15–30-cm) saucer-shaped flowers on 3–6-ft (90-cm–1.8-m) plants with broad leaves. Blooming from midsummer to autumn, the flowers may be white or shades of pink or red. Use as a specimen plant or accent in flower beds or among shrubs. A number of hybrid cultivars are also available. Scarlet rose mallow (*H. coccineus*) grows 6–8 ft (1.8–2.4 m) tall with fine-textured blue-green leaves and 6-in (15-cm) crimson flowers.

■ **CULTIVATION AND CARE TIPS.** They grow best in full sun with humus-rich, moist soil. Light shade and drier soil are tolerated once plants are established. Long-lived and resenting disturbance, they are also slow to sprout in the spring. Set plants 3 ft (90 cm) apart. Hardy to −20°F (−28°C), but in areas with a low of 0°F (−18°C) or less, a winter mulch is desirable.

■ **PROPAGATION.** Although seldom necessary, division in spring, setting the leaf buds 4 in (10 cm) deep. Cuttings. Seed.

■ **PESTS AND DISEASES.** Aphids; mealy bugs. Bud drop may develop if soil too dry or night temperature too low.

HOSTA

PLANTAIN LILY, FUNKIA

ONE OF THE MOST POPULAR and widely used of perennials, plantain lilies are chosen for their adaptability to various climates and soils, low-maintenance and the attractiveness of the neat, symmetrical mounds of leaves of varying textures and colours. Besides the numerous species, thousands of hybrid cultivars have been developed, ranging in size from less than 6 in (15 cm) to over 3 ft (90 cm) across, and often with variegated leaves. Although plantain lilies have spikes of white, purple, or lavender flowers in summer or autumn, some of which are fragrant, they are mainly grown as foliage plants. Use plantain lilies as specimens or in small groups in beds or borders, edging paths, or massed as a ground cover.

Hostas

■ **SPECIES, VARIETIES AND CULTIVARS.** Blunt-leaf plantain lily (*Hosta decorata*, also listed as 'Thomas Hogg') grows 2 ft (60 cm) tall with 6-in (15-cm) leaves rimmed in white and dark lavender flowers in August. Fortune's plantain lily (*H. fortunei*) grows 2 ft (60 cm) tall, with 5–8-in (12.5–20-cm) heart-shaped, grey-green leaves and lavender flowers in midsummer.

Narrow plantain lily (*H. lancifolia*) grows 2 ft (60 cm) tall and as wide with narrow, glossy, dark green leaves 4–6 in (1–15 cm) long and white-violet flowers in late summer and early autumn.

Fragrant plantain lily (*H. plantaginea*) is an old-fashioned favourite with large, fragrant white flowers in late summer, 10-in (25-cm), heart-shaped leaves forming plants 3 ft (90 cm) wide.

Siebold's plantain lily (*H. sieboldiana*) grows 30 in (75 cm) tall and twice as wide with 10–15-in (25–38-cm) long heart-shaped, blue-green puckered leaves and lavender flowers on short, partly hidden stalks bloom in summer.

Autumn plantain lily (*H. tardifolia*) grows 12 in (30 cm) tall with narrow, dark green leaves and deep purple flowers in late autumn. Wavy-leaf plantain lily (*H. undulata*) has pointed leaves 6 in (15 cm) long striped in white or cream with lavender flowers on 3 ft (90 cm) stalks in midsummer.

Blue plantain lily (*H. ventricosa*) has large glossy, dark green heart-shaped leaves and tall spikes of purple flowers in late summer and early autumn. 'Variegata' has dark green leaves strikingly variegated with yellow.

■ **CULTIVATION AND CARE TIPS.** They do best in light to deep shade and humus-rich, moist but well-drained soil. Wet soil in winter is very detrimental. Full sun is tolerated if soil is kept moist during the growing season, but variegated types may be less colourful. Remove faded bloom stalks from plantings when feasible. Set plants 1–2 ft (30–60 cm) apart, depending on mature size. Hardy to −30°F (−34°C).

■ **PROPAGATION.** Division of young plants in spring for increase only, otherwise leave undisturbed.

■ **PESTS AND DISEASES.** Slugs.

IBERIS

CANDYTUFT

ONE OF THE BEST spring-blooming plants, the 2-in (5-cm) clusters of white blooms of candytuft (*Iberis sempervirens*) are set off by the dense, fine-textured, dark evergreen leaves on creeping woody plants 6–10 in (15–25 cm) tall and 2 ft (60 cm) wide. It is excellent in a rock garden, tumbling over walls, at the front of beds and borders, as an edging, or in planters. There are a number of cultivars available, including 'Little Gem' and 'Snowflake'.

■ **CULTIVATION AND CARE TIPS.** It grows best in full sun with a humus-rich, neutral to alkaline, moist but well-drained soil. Prune stems back halfway after flowering to keep the plant bushy. Once well-established, leave undisturbed and it will be long-lived. Set plants 15 in (38 cm) apart. Hardy to −30°F (−34°C).

■ **PROPAGATION.** Cuttings in early summer. Divisions in early summer after flowering.

■ **PESTS AND DISEASES.** Flea beetles.

Iberis sempervirens

IRIS

IRIS

THOUSANDS OF VARIETIES in almost every colour except red, coupled with the sheer beauty of the unusually-shaped blooms, have made irises a garden favourite for centuries. Flowers consist of three upright petals called standards and three drooping petals called falls. Flowers may be bicoloured, and petals may be frilled, ruffled, or edged in a different colour; a crest or beard may decorate the centre of the falls. Flowering is usually in spring or summer, with a few cultivars of the tall bearded iris repeat-blooming in the autumn. Foliage is narrow, stiff, and sword-shaped, and plants grow by spreading, fleshy, rhizomatous roots. Use the shorter irises in a rock garden or at the front of flower beds and borders. Japanese irises are ideal planted at the edge of streams or in other moist areas. Taller irises can be planted in the middle to back of flower beds and borders, along a wall or among shrubs. Irises are superb cut flowers.

■ **SPECIES, VARIETIES AND CULTIVARS.** The most familiar irises are the bearded hybrids (often grouped under the heading *Iris germanica*), which are divided into dwarf, intermediate and tall classes, with further subdivisions according to flower size. Height ranges from 8 to 30 in (20 to 75 cm) and flowers from 1½ to 8 in (4 to 20 cm).

The long-lived Siberian iris (*I. sibirica*) is the easiest one to grow. Plants reach 3 ft (90 cm) tall with graceful, slender leaves and 3-in (7.5-cm) flowers in shades of white, blue, purple, red-purple, and violet. They bloom in summer after the bearded irises. Scatter clumps throughout flower beds and borders, as they tolerate

Iris ensata 'ELEANOR PARRY'

Iris sibirica

both full sun and light shade. Leave seed pods on the plants or cut for dried arrangements.

Japanese iris (*I. ensata*) grows 3–4 ft (90 cm–1.2 m) tall with flat, 6-in (15-cm) flowers in shades of white, blue, rose and purple in midsummer.

Crested iris (*I. cristata*) is one of the smaller irises, growing just 6 in (15 cm) tall with pale lavender-blue or white flowers in spring.

Roof iris (*I. tectorum*) grows 8–12 in (20–30 cm) tall with lavender-blue or white 3-in (7.5-cm) flowers. It grows in both full sun and light shade.

■ **CULTIVATION AND CARE TIPS.** Unless otherwise noted, they grow best in full sun but tolerate light shade. Bearded, crested, Siberian, and roof irises need a humus-rich, moist but well-drained soil with the rhizomes 1 in (2.5 cm) below the soil surface. Japanese irises prefer humus-rich, constantly moist soils. Siberian and roof irises do best with slightly acid soil. Except as noted, deadhead regularly. Set shorter types 12 in (30 cm) apart and taller types 18 in (45 cm) apart. Hardy to −20°F (−28°C).

■ **PROPAGATION.** Division of rhizomes after flowering. Bearded iris usually need dividing every three or four years.

■ **PESTS AND DISEASES.** Prone to a number including iris borer followed by bacterial soft rot, evidenced by trails of slime along leaf edges. Begin spraying in spring and repeat weekly for three weeks; remove and destroy infected rhizomes at any time, and old foliage in the autumn to prevent overwintering borer eggs.

KNIPHOFIA

TORCH LILY, RED HOT POKER

Dense mounds of gracefully arching grey-green leaves yield stiff spikes of bright orange, red, cream, coral, or yellow flowers for a long period in summer. The hybrids bloom in midsummer and the species in late summer and early autumn. Foliage grows 12–30 in (30–75 cm) tall and the flower spikes reach 2–4 ft (60 cm–1.2 m) tall.

Torch lilies are long-lived and are best used as individual accent plants or in groups of three in the front to middle of flower beds and borders. The flowers are good for cutting.

■ **SPECIES, VARIETIES AND CULTIVARS.** The species (*K. uvaria*, also listed as *K. pfitzeri* or *Tritoma uvaria*) is hardy to 0°F (−18°C), but the various hybrid cultivars are hardy to −20°F (−28°C), especially with a loose winter mulch of evergreen branches or leaves.

■ **CULTIVATION AND CARE TIPS.** They grow well in full sun with humus-rich, moist but well-drained soil. Wet soil in winter is usually fatal. Avoid windy sites as plants are difficult to stake. Set plants 18 in (45 cm) apart, planting in spring.

■ **PROPAGATION.** Division in early spring every four or five years, if desired, removing young side growths or digging the entire plant and separating.

■ **PESTS AND DISEASES.** Thrips.

Kniphofia HYBRID

Lavandula angustifolia

LAVANDULA

LAVENDER

An old-fashioned garden favourite, lavender is beloved for the scent of its flowers and leaves as well as for its effectiveness as a specimen plant in beds, borders, and rock gardens, and as an edging or low hedge. Needle-like, grey-green leaves and lavender, purple, pink, or white flowers provide a fine-textured, softly blending plant for the garden. Flowers are produced from early to late summer, and they can be used in fresh arrangements or dried for use in potpourri and sachets. Lavender (*L. angustifolia*, also listed as *L. officinalis, L. vera,* or *L. spica*) grows 1–3 ft (30–90 cm) tall.

■ **CULTIVATION AND CARE TIPS.** It needs full sun and sandy, alkaline, well-drained soil that is not too fertile. Prune back old wood in the spring. Set plants 12 in (30 cm) apart. Hardy to −20°F (−28°C). A winter mulch in climates of 0°F (−18°C) or colder is necessary.

■ **PROPAGATION.** Cuttings in early summer. Seed.

■ **PESTS AND DISEASES.** Froghoppers; leaf spot.

Linum perenne

LIATRIS

GAYFEATHER, BLAZING STAR

TALL, NARROW WANDS of purple, magenta, or white small, fluffy flowers, excellent for attracting butterflies, bloom from midsummer to early autumn. Superb for cutting and using fresh or dried, the flowers are unusual in that they open from the top downwards. The stiff, narrow, dark green foliage forms grassy tufts that have a fine-textured appearance. Utilize the strong vertical effect of gayfeather towards the middle of flower beds and borders or in meadow gardens.

■ **SPECIES, VARIETIES AND CULTIVARS.** *Liatris pycnostachya* grows 4–5 ft (1.2–1.5 m) tall with 1-in (2.5-cm) rosy-lavender flowers in late summer and early autumn. Spiked gayfeather (*L. spicata*) has stems densely covered with leaves and deep magenta or white ½-in (12-mm) flowers in late summer. Plants grow 3 ft (90 cm) tall.

■ **CULTIVATION AND CARE TIPS.** Long-lived, they grow well in full sun with sandy to average, moist but well-drained soils. Tolerant of dry soil, they must have good winter drainage. Staking may be required. Deadhead to prevent self-sowing. Set plants 12–18 in (30–45 cm) apart. Hardy to −40°F (−40°C).

■ **PROPAGATION.** Division of crowded plants every three or four years in early spring. Seed.

■ **PESTS AND DISEASES.** Slugs.

Liatris spicata

LINUM

FLAX

PERENNIAL FLAX FORMS graceful, upright clumps with small, fine-textured leaves and delicate-looking flowers of blue, yellow, or white. Each bloom lasts only a day, but if kept picked, plants bloom all summer. Use flax in the front or middle of beds, borders and in rock gardens. Blue flax is also good in meadow gardens.

■ **SPECIES, VARIETIES AND CULTIVARS.** Blue flax (*Linum perenne*) grows 18–24 in (45–60 cm) tall with blue-green leaves and clear-blue or white 1-in (2.5-cm) flowers. Narbonne flax (*L. narbonense*) has 1-in (2.5-cm) azure-blue flowers with white centres on plants 18–24 in (45–60 cm) tall. Golden flax (*L. flavum*) grows 12–18 in (30–45 cm) tall with green leaves and bright yellow 1-in (2.5-cm) flowers.

■ **CULTIVATION AND CARE TIPS.** It grows best in full sun with sandy to average, moist but well-drained soil. Set plants 18 in (45 cm) apart. Protect the shallow roots with a mulch. Hardy to −20°F (−28°C).

■ **PROPAGATION.** Seed. Cuttings. Division in early spring.

■ **PESTS AND DISEASES.** Seldom bothered.

LOBELIA

CARDINAL FLOWER, GREAT BLUE LOBELIA

WITH THE RIGHT GROWING conditions, both species can offer intensely coloured spikes of asymmetrical flowers from summer to autumn above low-growing clumps of leaves. They are effective when planted beside streams, in meadow gardens, lightly shaded beds or borders.

■ **SPECIES, VARIETIES AND CULTIVARS.** Cardinal flower (*Lobelia cardinalis*) has 1½-in (4-cm) scarlet red flowers on spikes 3–4 ft (90 cm–1.2 m) tall. Hardy to −50°F (−46°C). Great blue lobelia (*L. siphilitica*) has 1-in (2.5-cm) dark blue flowers on 2–3-ft (60–90-cm) stems. Hardy to −20°F (−28°C). There are hybrid cultivars of both species.

■ **CULTIVATION AND CARE TIPS.** Both species grow best in light shade but tolerate full sun if the soil is always moist. A wet or moist, humus-rich soil is preferable. Staking may be needed. Although not always long-lived, they readily self-sow with the right growing conditions. Mulching keeps soil moist, improves hardiness, and encourages seedlings to grow. Set plants 12–18 in (30–45 cm) apart.

■ **PROPAGATION.** Seed. Remove and replant offsets in early autumn.

■ **PESTS AND DISEASES.** Rhizoctonia; stem rot. A virus disease affects cardinal flowers.

Lobelia cardinalis

Lupinus x 'RUSSELL HYBRIDS'

LUPINUS

LUPIN

LUPINS (*Lupinus* × 'Russell Hybrids') have showy 2–3-ft (60–90-cm) spikes of 1-in (2.5-cm) pea-like flowers in shades of white, yellow, pink, red, blue or purple, either solid or bicolored, in early summer. The bushy plants have hand-shaped grey or bright green leaves. Lupins grow best in areas with cool, moist summers, and planted in the middle, centre or back of flower beds and borders. They usually live about four years and do not readily transplant once established.

■ **CULTIVATION AND CARE TIPS.** They do well with either full sun or light shade and need humus-rich, moist but well-drained soil. Set plants 18–24 in (45–60 cm) apart. Deadhead regularly to promote second flowering. Mulch to conserve moisture and provide winter protection. Hardy to −20°F (−28°C).

■ **PROPAGATION.** Seed, which must be nicked with a file to germinate readily. Stem cuttings, with a portion of the root attached, in spring.

■ **PESTS AND DISEASES.** Crown and root rot; honey fungus; powdery mildew; mosaic and other virus diseases.

Lychnis chalcedonica

LYCHNIS

MALTESE CROSS, ROSE CAMPION, GERMAN CATCHFLY

THE VARIOUS species are useful in the front to middle of flower beds and borders or naturalized in meadow gardens. The flowers are good for cutting.

■ **SPECIES, VARIETIES AND CULTIVARS.** The various species of lychnis suitable for the garden are very different in appearance. Maltese cross (*L. chalcedonica*) forms dense clumps with straight stems growing 2–3 ft (60–90 cm) tall with hairy, dark green leaves and clusters of 1-in (2.5-cm) orange-scarlet flowers from early to mid-summer. A second blooming occurs if faded flowers are removed. Plants are short-lived, but they readily reseed. Staking may be necessary.

Rose campion (*L. coronaria*) is a biennial with woolly, silvery-grey stems and leaves. Open and branching, the plants grow 18–24 in (45–60 cm) tall with 1-in (2.5-cm) magenta flowers, which attract butterflies. Plants readily reseed. Different forms are available.

Longer-lived German catchfly (*L. viscaria*) has hummocks of grassy, semi-evergreen foliage and slender 12–18-in (30–45-cm) stems that are sticky just beneath the bunches of ½-in (12-mm) flowers that bloom from late spring to midsummer. Different forms are available.

■ **CULTIVATION AND CARE TIPS.** The plants tolerate drought and grow best in full sun in average, very well-drained soil. Wet soil in winter is often fatal. Set plants 12 in (30 cm) apart. Hardy to −40°F (−40°C).

■ **PROPAGATION.** Seed. Division in spring or autumn, usually every three or four years.

■ **PESTS AND DISEASES.** Aphids; froghoppers. Maltese cross may develop a virus disease.

Lychnis coronaria

Lysimachia clethroides

JAPANESE LOOSESTRIFE, YELLOW LOOSESTRIFE

JAPANESE LOOSESTRIFE (*L. clethroides*) and yellow loosestrife (*L. punctata*) are very different in appearance, but share the common trait of being ideal for naturalizing beside streams or in other large, sunny or lightly shaded areas, as the roots tend to spread rapidly.

■ **SPECIES, VARIETIES AND CULTIVARS.** Japanese loosestrife grows 2–3 ft (60–90 cm) tall. Good for cutting, the ½-in (12-mm) white flowers are in narrow spikes that curve gracefully to one side. Blooming continues throughout summer and foliage colours a bronze-yellow in the autumn. Yellow loosestrife is the same height, but the 1-in (2.5-cm) yellow flowers are set in the axils where the leaves join the upright stems. Plants bloom from early to midsummer.

■ **CULTIVATION AND CARE TIPS.** Both types grow in average to humus-rich, moist soil. Drier soil is tolerated in light shade. Set plants 12 in (30 cm) apart from each other or 3 ft (90 cm) from other plants to allow the root to spread. Hardy to −30°F (−34°C).

■ **PROPAGATION.** Division in late autumn or early spring. Seed.

■ **PESTS AND DISEASES.** Seldom bothered.

PURPLE LOOSESTRIFE

VARYING WIDELY IN HEIGHT and flower colour, purple loosestrife is a very adaptable, low-maintenance, bushy plant that blooms from early summer until autumn. Foliage is small and willow-like, providing fine texture in the garden, and the spikes of ¾-in (18-mm) flowers are produced abundantly.

■ **SPECIES, VARIETIES AND CULTIVARS.** Purple loosestrife (*Lythrum salicaria*) has become widely naturalized by self-sowing. Many cultivars are available that have better colour and are seemingly sterile and therefore not invasive. Most grow 3 ft (90 cm) tall.

■ **CULTIVATION AND CARE TIPS.** Although they naturally grow in wet meadows and beside streams, they also do well in moist, well-drained soil and even withstand dry conditions. Full sun is best, but light shade is tolerated. Set plants 18 in (45 cm) apart. Hardy to −40°F (−40°C).

■ **PROPAGATION.** Division in spring or autumn. Root cuttings in early summer.

■ **PESTS AND DISEASES.** Seldom bothered.

Lythrum salicaria

Macleaya cordata

MACLEAYA

PLUME POPPY

BEST USED AS A specimen plant near a building or hedge, plume poppy (*Macleaya cordata*, also listed as *Bocconia cordata*) is bold and dramatic with its rounded, scalloped blue-green leaves with silvery undersides on 6–10-ft (1.8–3-m) stems. Fluffy, 12-in (30-cm) plumes of ½-in (12-mm) petal-less flowers bloom during summer, and the seed pods are attractive until frost. Both can be cut and dried for arrangements. Plants readily self-sow.

■ **CULTIVATION AND CARE TIPS.** It grows best in light shade in hotter regions, but full sun is tolerated in cooler areas. Plant in average moist to well-drained soil, spacing 3–4 ft (90 cm–1.2 m) apart. Hardy to −30°F (−34°C).

■ **PROPAGATION.** Division in spring. Seed.

■ **PESTS AND DISEASES.** Seldom bothered.

MARRUBIUM

HOREHOUND

ALTHOUGH USUALLY CONSIDERED for the herb garden, silver horehound (*Marrubium incanum*, also listed as *M. candidissimum*) is a good choice for flower beds and borders because it is one of the few silver-grey perennials that does not quickly rot in hot, humid climates. The wrinkled, woolly leaves are up to 2 in (5 cm) long on plants growing 2–3 ft (60–90 cm) tall and wide. The ⅛-in (3-mm) flowers are white and in rondels along the stems; remove unless self-sowing is desired, as the plant can become invasive.

■ **CULTIVATION AND CARE TIPS.** Drought-tolerant, it grows best in full sun with sandy, well-drained soil. Plants sprawl in rich, moist soil; control by shearing back when 12 in (30 cm) tall. Set plants 12 in (30 cm) apart. Hardy to −30°F (−34°C).

■ **PROPAGATION.** Seed. Division, if plants are not too woody.

■ **PESTS AND DISEASES.** Seldom bothered.

Marrubium incanum

Mertensia virginica

MERTENSIA

VIRGINIA COWSLIP

A BELOVED SPRING-BLOOMING wild flower, Virginia cowslip (*M. virginica*) is best grown in drifts under trees at the edge of a lawn. The foliage dies back in summer, so it is preferable to interplant with other plants. It grows 1–2 ft (30–60 cm) tall with oval, blue-green leaves and nodding clusters of 1-in (2.5-cm) fragrant, funnel-shaped flowers that are pinkish in bud, then becoming blue as they open. There are also pink- and white-flowered forms. Plants readily reseed.

■ **CULTIVATION AND CARE TIPS.** They grow best in light to full shade with acid, humus-rich, moist but well-drained soil that is drier when plants are dormant. Set plants 8–12 in (20–30 cm) apart, with the crown 1 in (2.5 cm) deep. Hardy to −30°F (−34°C).

■ **PROPAGATION.** Seed sown as soon as ripe. Division in autumn.

■ **PESTS AND DISEASES.** Seldom bothered.

Monarda didyma 'CAMBRIDGE SCARLET'

MONARDA

Bee Balm, Wild Bergamot

Long-lived, easily grown, and adaptable, bee balm (*Monarda didyma*) blooms for much of the summer with unusually shaped flowers in shades of white, pink, lavender, magenta, red or burgundy. Excellent for cutting, the 2–3-in (5–7.5-cm) flowers attract bees. The dark green leaves have a minty scent, and both flowers and leaves can be dried for adding to potpourris. It is a superb choice for the middle to back of borders or centre of beds as well as for naturalizing as they spread by runners. Growing to 2–3 ft (60–90 cm) tall with slightly hairy foliage, a number of named cultivars are available. Wild bergamot (*M. fistulosa*) grows 3–4 ft (90 cm–1.2 m) tall with softly hairy leaves and lavender to purple 1½-in (4-cm) flowers. It can be invasive, so is best grown in naturalized areas.

■ **CULTIVATION AND CARE TIPS.** Both bee balm and wild bergamot readily grow in both full sun and light shade, with more soil moisture necessary in full sun positions. A wide range of soils are tolerated, but a humus-rich, moist but well-drained soil is best preferred. Wild bergamot, however, is more tolerant of poorer, drier soil and hotter summers than bee balm. Deadhead regularly to encourage additional flowering through the summer. Cut plants back to the ground in the autumn. When planting out, set plants 18 in (45 cm) apart. Hardy to −30°F (−34°C).

■ **PROPAGATION.** Division in spring every three or four years. Seed for the species.

■ **PESTS AND DISEASES.** Seldom bothered.

Oenothera tetragona

NEPETA

CATMINT

RELATED TO CATNIP, two very similar types of cat-mint are lovely in the garden because their delicate texture and colour blend so readily with other flowers and plants. The sprawling mounds are useful as an edging, in a rock garden, in raised beds or walls, or at the front of beds and borders. Small, heart-shaped, hairy grey leaves densely cover the 12–18-in (30–45-cm) plants. Spikes of ¼-in (6-mm) softly coloured blue or white flowers in spring and early summer may rebloom if plants are cut back by half after the first blooming.

■ **SPECIES, VARIETIES AND CULTIVARS.** *N. × faassenii* is sterile and does not self-sow so plants must be propagated by division. *N. mussinii* can be raised from seed. 'Six Hills Giant' is a good cultivar.

■ **CULTIVATION AND CARE TIPS.** They grow best in full sun in sandy, well-drained soil. Plants have more compact, attractive growth in poor soil and are tolerant of drought and hot summers. Set plants 12–18 in (30–45 cm) apart. Hardy to −40°F (−40°C).

■ **PROPAGATION.** Both types may be divided in spring. Seed for *N. mussinii*.

■ **PESTS AND DISEASES.** Powdery mildew.

Nepeta × faassenii

OENOTHERA

EVENING OR MISSOURI PRIMROSE

BEAUTIFUL PINK OR YELLOW fragrant flowers, blooming for much of the summer, have made these perennials popular for rock gardens, as an edging, or at the front of beds and borders.

■ **SPECIES, VARIETIES AND CULTIVARS.** What is purchased as *Oenothera fruticosa* var. *youngii* may be *O. tetragona* as they are similar. They grow 18–24 in (45–60 cm) tall with narrow, shiny green leaves and 1-in (2.5-cm) saucer-shaped, yellow flowers blooming during the day. The evening or Missouri primrose (*O. missourensis*) has trailing stems 12 in (30 cm) long and yellow flowers 4 in (10 cm) across, which open in the evening and remain so until the following evening. The seed pods can be dried for bouquets. The showy primrose (*O. speciosa*) grows 18 in (45 cm) tall with 2-in (5-cm) pink or white flowers. It can become invasive so choose the site carefully.

■ **CULTIVATION AND CARE TIPS.** All species are easily grown in full sun with average well-drained soil. They are tolerant of poor, dry conditions and heat. Set plants 18 in (45 cm) apart. Hardy to −20°F (−28°C).

■ **PROPAGATION.** Seed. Division in spring every three or four years.

■ **PESTS AND DISEASES.** Eelworms; root rot; mildew.

Ornamental Grasses

ORNAMENTAL GRASSES offer the gardener wonderfully fine textures in a wide range of sizes, shapes and colours. They often also provide year-round interest because of the long-lasting seed-heads foliage that persists during the winter. They can be used in many different ways, in flower beds and borders, as specimens against walls, or among shrubs, massed in drifts, used as ground cover, or as part of a meadow garden. Many of the grass flowers are excellent for using fresh or dried in arrangements.

■ **SPECIES, VARIETIES AND CULTIVARS.** Very supple and graceful, feather reed grass (*Calamagrostis* × *acutiflora* 'Karl Foerster') has very thin pale green leaves 30 in (75 cm) tall and narrow flowers growing 5 ft (1.5 m) tall. These open pale gold in midsummer, turn brown by autumn, and persist in winter, shading to grey. Wild oats (*Chasmanthium latifolium*, also listed as *Uniola latifolia*) has broad, dark green leaves 2 ft (60 cm) tall and spread slowly to 3 ft (90 cm) across. Autumn-blooming, the golden-tan flowers are flattened spikes on wiry, arching stems. Light shade is tolerated. Blue wild rye (*Elymus glaucus*) has flat leaves growing 4 ft (1.2 m) tall with late-summer flowers. It spreads readily and is good as a ground cover. Divide every two to three years. Hardy to −50°F (−46°C). Blue fescue (*Festuca cinerea*, also listed as *F. ovina* 'Glauca') is a very fine-textured, spiky grass forming rounded clumps 8–10 in (20–25 cm) tall. Plants bloom in June, but these are best clipped off. Blue oat grass (*Helictotrichon sempervirens*) forms stiff, spiky clumps of fine-textured blue-green leaves 2 ft (60 cm) tall. Flower stems grow 4 ft (1.2 m) tall but are not particularly showy. Japanese

Pennisetum alopecuroides

blood grass (*Imperata cylindrica* 'Rubra') has broad, flat, spiky, 2-ft (60-cm) leaves of a striking deep red. It is useful among grey-leaved plants and in rock gardens. Hardy to −20°F (−28°C). There are a number of cultivars of eulalia grass (*Miscanthus sinensis*), with most having 5–7-ft (1.5–2.1-m) silken, feathery plumes in late summer that persist well through the winter, and graceful, arching foliage growing 4–6 ft (1.2–1.8 m) tall. Fountain grass (*Pennisetum alopecuroides*) has typical grassy foliage growing 30 in (75 cm) tall with an abundance of fuzzy, bottle-brush, 5-in (12.5-cm) flowers that are green in midsummer, changing to brown in autumn, and tan in winter. Ribbon grass (*Phalaris arundinacea* 'Picta') is a vigorous, spreading plant with green-and-white striped leaves growing 2–3 ft (60–90 cm) tall. Hardy to −40°F (−40°C).

■ **CULTIVATION AND CARE TIPS.** Of the dozens of ornamental grasses, the ones listed are most readily available and easiest to grow. They have similar requirements, including full sun and a humus-rich, moist but well-drained soil. Average to poor soil and dry conditions are usually tolerated. Trim plants back to ground level before growth begins in the spring. It may take several years for ornamental grasses to become fully established. Hardy to −30°F (−34°C) unless otherwise noted.

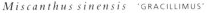

Miscanthus sinensis 'GRACILLIMUS'

Paeonia 'ANGELUS'

PAEONIA

PEONY

PEONIES ARE AMONG the most widely grown of perennials and will live for decades. Blooming in late spring and early summer, the bushy plants grow 2–3 ft (60–90 cm) tall with lush, shiny foliage. Use peonies in flower beds and borders, in front of shrubs, as a low hedge or beside a wall.

■ **SPECIES, VARIETIES AND CULTIVARS.** There are thousands of hybrid cultivars of the common, or Chinese, peony (*Paeonia lactiflora*). The 3–6-in (7.5–15-cm) wide blooms may be shades of white, creamy yellow, pink, or red and in one of five forms: single, with eight petals and a prominent cluster of yellow stamens; Japanese, with a carnation-like centre and a saucer-shaped petal collar; anemone, similar to Japanese but shaggier; semi-double, with stamens apparent; and double, with stamens missing or hidden. Excellent for cutting, the flowers of some varieties are fragrant. By choosing early, midseason, and late-blooming kinds, the blooming period can be extended for six weeks. *P. officinalis*, sometimes also called common peony, is similar to *P. lactiflora* with 4-in (10-cm) single crimson flowers with yellow stamens.

■ **CULTIVATION AND CARE TIPS.** All peonies are easily grown in humus-rich, moist but well-drained soil in full sun, or light shade in hotter areas. Set the eyes, or red sprouts, 1 in (2.5 cm) deep and 2–3 ft (60–90 cm) apart in fall before the ground freezes. Taller types may need staking. To prevent peony wilt, cut off all stems and leaves in autumn. Hardy to −40°F (−40°C), a mulch is beneficial in areas −20°F (−28°C) or colder with no snow cover. Winter chilling is necessary, and peonies do not grow and bloom well in subtropical areas.

■ **PROPAGATION.** Although best left undisturbed, peonies can be divided in autumn, cutting roots apart with a knife, with each piece having three eyes.

■ **PESTS AND DISEASES.** Swift moth caterpillars; honey fungus; leaf spot; peony wilt; mosaic.

Paeonia 'MONS. JULES ELIE'

Papaver orientale

PAPAVER

ORIENTAL POPPY

AN OLD-FASHIONED FAVOURITE, Oriental poppies (*P. orientale*) are beloved for the early summer blooming, papery translucent orange, red, pink, salmon or white flowers, often with a purple-black blotch in the centre. The silver-green, rough-textured, fern-like leaves and the 6-in (15-cm) flowers grow on plants 2–4 ft (60 cm–1.2 m) tall. The flowers are good for cutting if picked just as buds begin to open in early morning and the stem ends are seared in a flame. Plants go dormant after flowering, so they are best planted in beds or borders near other perennials. They are long-lived and best left undisturbed for at least five years.

■ **CULTIVATION AND CARE TIPS.** They are easily grown in full sun with average well-drained soil. Poor drainage in winter is usually fatal. Staking may be necessary with taller types. Set plants 18 in (45 cm) apart, with the crown 3 in (7.5 cm) deep. Hardy to −30°F (−34°C). Both a summer and winter mulch is beneficial.

■ **PROPAGATION.** Division in late summer or autumn when new growth appears. Root cuttings in late summer.

■ **PESTS AND DISEASES.** Downy mildew.

PHLOX

PHLOXES ARE A LARGE, diverse group of perennials that provide a wide range of sizes, shapes and colours. As such, they are indispensable in a garden. They are easily grown and bloom for long periods, with each type having the distinctive five-petalled, flat-faced flower. The taller types are best used in beds and borders; the shorter, creeping types in wild flower and woodland gardens; and the mat-forming ones spilling over the edges of raised beds, in walls or rock gardens.

■ **SPECIES, VARIETIES AND CULTIVARS.** Carolina phlox (*Phlox caroliniana*, also listed as *P. suffruticosa*) grows in clumps 3 ft (90 cm) tall with loose, somewhat flat clusters of ¾-in (18-mm) purple to pink flowers in early summer. Resistant to powdery mildew, it is also tolerant of light shade.

Wild sweet william (*P. divaricata*) grows 12 in (30 cm) tall with rapidly spreading creeping stems. The 1-in (2.5-cm) light blue, lavender or white flowers bloom in loose, flat clusters in early spring. It grows best in light shade.

Meadow phlox (*P. maculata*, but sometimes listed as *P. caroliniana*, which it resembles) grows in clumps with strong 2–4-ft (60-cm–1.2-m) stems and large clusters of fragrant, ½-in (12-mm) purple, pink or white flowers. Resistant to mildew and seldom requiring staking, cutting back encourages a second bloom.

Phlox divaricata 'CHATTAHOOCHEE'

Phlox paniculata

Garden phlox (*P. paniculata*) grows in clumps 3–4 ft (90 cm–1.2 m) tall and blooms from summer to early autumn with large, open clusters of 1-in (2.5-cm) flowers in shades of pink, white, red or pale blue. They are temperamental plant, susceptible to mildew, and do best in cool-summer areas.

Creeping phlox (*P. stolonifera*) grows 12 in (30 cm) tall with creeping stems. The spring-blooming ¾-in (18-mm) flowers may be purple, violet or blue.

Ground, or moss, pink (*P. subulata*) is a mat-forming plant growing 6 in (15 cm) high with needle-like leaves. It is densely covered with bright purple, pink or white, ¾-in (18-mm) flowers in early spring.

■ **CULTIVATION AND CARE TIPS.** They grow best in humus-rich, moist but well-drained soil. Set plants 12–24 in (30–60 cm) apart. Hardy to −40°F (−40°C).

■ **PROPAGATION.** Division in spring, usually every three or four years. Cuttings.

■ **PESTS AND DISEASES.** Eelworms; slugs; leaf spot; leafy gall; powdery mildew.

OBEDIENT PLANT

EASY TO GROW, obedient plant (*Physostegia virginiana*, also listed as *Dracocephalum virginianum*) grows in bushy clumps 2–4 ft (60 cm–1.2 m) tall with stiff, wand-like spikes of pink, magenta, rose, lilac, or white tubular 1-in (2.5-cm) flowers. Blooming for a long time in summer and autumn, the flowers are excellent for cutting. It spreads rapidly and is useful in wild flower gardens and beside streams. The named cultivars are better for more formal areas of the garden, such as traditional beds and borders.

■ **CULTIVATION AND CARE TIPS.** It grows best in full sun with average, moist, slightly acid soil. Drier soil is tolerated, especially in light shade, but plants will be shorter. Set plants 18–24 in (45–60 cm) apart. Hardy to −40°F (−40°C).

■ **PROPAGATION.** Division in spring every other year.

■ **PESTS AND DISEASES.** Seldom bothered.

Physostegia virginiana

Polygonatum odoratum thunbergii 'VARIEGATUM'

PLATYCODON

BALLOON FLOWER

FORMING 18–30-in (45–75-cm) tall, stiffly bushy plants, balloon flower (*Platycodon grandiflorum*) derives its common name from the shape of the bud, which opens into a 2-in (5-cm), cup-like, star-shaped blue flower. This long-blooming perennial also has many other varieties. Flowers are beautiful in arrangements; stem ends must be seared in a flame.

■ **CULTIVATION AND CARE TIPS.** This easily grown, adaptable plant does not start to sprout until late in the spring, so the location must be marked well. Blue- and white-flowered cultivars thrive in full sun, but pink flowers fade unless in light shade. Provide average to sandy, well-drained soil; poor drainage in winter is fatal. The plants may take several years to become established, and if moved, must be dug deeply to get all of the long roots, which spread slowly. Division is seldom necessary and the plants are long-lived. Plants also self-sow, but not rampantly. Staking is necessary with taller cultivars. Deadhead regularly to prolong blooming. Set plants 12–18 in (30–45 cm) apart, with the crown just below the soil surface; a group of three plants in the middle of a bed or border is most effective. Although hardy to −40°F (−40°C), some loose winter protection is often necessary for plants to survive.

■ **PROPAGATION.** Cut off outer sections of crown in spring when shoots are 1 in (2.5 cm) tall. Seed.

■ **PESTS AND DISEASES.** Seldom bothered.

Platycodon grandiflorum

POLYGONATUM

SOLOMON'S SEAL

THE DIFFERENT FORMS OF Solomon's seal are all similar in appearance, with arching, unbranched stems of pointed, oval leaves and drooping, tubular, white or cream flowers in late spring and early summer.

■ **SPECIES, VARIETIES AND CULTIVARS.** Mainly grown as handsome foliage plants for light to full shade, *Polygonatum biflorum* grows 1–3 ft (30–90 cm) tall, *P. commutatum* (also listed as *P. giganteum*) 4–6 ft (1.2–1.8 m) tall, and *P. × hybridum* (also listed as *P. multiflorum*) 3 ft (90 cm) tall. The variegated Japanese Solomon's seal (*P. odoratum thunbergii* 'Variegatum') growing 2–3 ft (60–90 cm) tall with leaves edged in creamy white, is considered the most beautiful form.

■ **CULTIVATION AND CARE TIPS.** The rhizomatous roots spread slowly forming handsome colonies. Long-lived, it is seldom invasive and division is rarely needed. It thrives in humus-rich, moist but well-drained soil; dry soil is however tolerated. Set plants 18–24 in (45–60 cm) apart. Hardy to −30°F (−34°C).

■ **PROPAGATION.** Division in spring or autumn. Seed.

■ **PESTS AND DISEASES.** Seldom bothered.

PRIMULA

PRIMROSE

HUNDREDS OF SPECIES and thousands of cultivars of primrose have captured the hearts of gardeners for the bright colours they bring to a lightly shaded spring garden. Most types form a ground-hugging clump with long, narrow or rounded, oval leaves and leafless stalks bearing clusters of five-petalled, semidouble, or double flowers. Although generally short-lived, primroses are readily started from seed.

■ **SPECIES, VARIETIES AND CULTIVARS.** The alpine primrose (*Primula auricula*) grows 8 in (20 cm) tall with clusters of fragrant, spring-blooming, 1-in (2.5-cm) flowers in a wide range of muted colours with a white eye. Hybrid forms are more easily grown than the species. Hardy to −40°F (−40°C). The drumstick primrose (*P. denticulata*) has rounded, 2-in (5-cm) heads of lilac flowers in spring on 10-in (25-cm) stems. Hardy to −30°F (−34°C). The Japanese primrose (*P. japonica*) has whorls of 1-in (2.5-cm) magenta, crimson, pink or white flowers spaced at intervals along stalks growing 2 ft (60 cm) tall. It readily self-seeds, especially if grown in constantly moist soil, such as on banks of streams. Hardy to −20°F (−28°C). Most widely grown of all primroses is the polyanthus primrose (*P.* × *polyantha*), which grows 10 in (25 cm) tall with single or

Primula denticulata

double, 1–2-in (2.5–5-cm) flowers in almost every conceivable colour. Generally hardy to −30°F (−34°C), but this depends on the cultivar. Siebold primrose (*P. sieboldii*) has crinkly, scalloped leaves with clusters of pink, rose or white, 1–2-in (2.5–5-cm) flowers in late spring and early summer on 12-in (30-cm) plants. It is somewhat tolerant of hot conditions. Hardy to −20°F (−28°C). English, or common, primrose (*P. vulgaris*, also listed as *P. acaulis*) has lightly fragrant, 1-in (2.5-cm), yellow flowers in early spring on 6-in (15-cm) plants with evergreen leaves. There are a number of cultivars and strains in a wide range of other colours. Hardy to −20°F (−28°C).

■ **CULTIVATION AND CARE TIPS.** Most types grow best with high, light shade and humus-rich, moist but well-drained soil. A summer mulch and watering during dry periods is necessary. A loose winter mulch is beneficial in cold areas with minimal snow cover. Set plants 12 in (30 cm) apart.

■ **PROPAGATION.** Division after flowering. Seed.

■ **PESTS AND DISEASES.** Aphids; caterpillars; brown core; root rot; grey mould; leaf spot; rust.

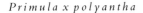

Primula x polyantha

Pulmonaria saccharata 'MISS MOON'

PULMONARIA
LUNGWORT, BETHLEHEM SAGE

SMALL, CREEPING PLANTS with hairy, dark green or mottled leaves and spring-blooming pink, blue or white flowers, the subtlety of pulmonarias is best appreciated when they are grown at the front of a shady border, as an edging to a path, or planted in drifts among shrubs and trees. The foliage is attractive throughout the growing season.

■ **SPECIES, VARIETIES AND CULTIVARS.** Blue lungwort (*Pulmonaria angustifolia*) grows 6–12 inches (15–30 cm) tall with narrow, dark green leaves. Dense clusters of pink buds open to ½-in (12-mm) blue flowers. Bethlehem sage (*P. saccharata*) grows 12–18 in (30–45 cm) tall with semi-evergreen leaves mottled with grey or white spots. The clusters of ½-in (12-mm) flowers may be white, blue or pink.

■ **CULTIVATION AND CARE TIPS.** They grow best in light shade with a humus-rich, moist but well-drained soil. Set plants 12 in (30 cm) apart. Division is seldom necessary unless plants become overcrowded, and plants are not invasive. Hardy to −30°F (−34°C).

■ **PROPAGATION.** Division in autumn.

■ **PESTS AND DISEASES.** Sawfly.

RUDBECKIA
CONEFLOWER, BLACK-EYED SUSAN

THE BOLD, BRIGHT golden-yellow, daisy-like flowers blooming from midsummer to autumn have made the various coneflowers popular for generations of gardeners. Some are annuals, biennials or short-lived perennials, but two are long-lived, low-maintenance perennials useful for the front to the middle of beds and borders, massed in large drifts or planted in meadow gardens. Flowers are good for cutting, and the dark cones remaining after the flowers have faded are eye-catching in the winter garden.

■ **SPECIES, VARIETIES AND CULTIVARS.** Orange coneflower, or black-eyed Susan (*Rudbeckia fulgida*), forms 2–3-ft (60–90-cm) tall bushy, branching plants with hairy leaves and 3–4-in (7.5–10-cm) flowers with yellow-orange petals surrounding a brown-black cone. The popular cultivar *R. fulgida* var. *sullivantii* 'Goldsturm' grows 2 ft (60 cm) tall and produces masses of large flowers. *R. nitida* grows 3–4 ft (90 cm–1.2 m) tall with lemon-yellow flowers with greenish centres. 'Herbstone' is a dramatic form.

■ **CULTIVATION AND CARE TIPS.** They readily grow in full sun and average to moist, well-drained soil. Set 18 in (45 cm) apart. Hardy to −40°F (−40°C).

■ **PROPAGATION.** Division in early spring every three or four years. Seed.

■ **PESTS AND DISEASES.** Slugs; snails.

Rudbeckia fulgida

SALVIA

THE GENUS *Salvia* is a very large one, with annual, biennial and perennial forms, including the popular annual scarlet salvia as well as the culinary herb sage. The longest-lived perennial sage, easiest to grow and best for low-maintenance gardens, is violet sage (*Salvia × superba*, also listed as *S. nemorosa*), which has an abundance of 6–12-in (15–30-cm) stalks of dark purple, ½-in (12-mm) flowers. These are good for fresh or dried arrangements. Plants grow 18–36 in (45–90 cm) tall with grey-green leaves.

■ **CULTIVATION AND CARE TIPS.** It does best with full sun and average, well-drained soil, and is tolerant of drought. Poorly drained soil in winter is usually fatal. Set plants 12–18 in (30–45 cm) apart. Deadhead regularly to prolong blooming. Although hardy to −20°F (−28°C), a loose winter mulch is beneficial.

■ **PROPAGATION.** Division in spring or autumn.

■ **PESTS AND DISEASES.** Red spider mites. Physiological disorder in young plants caused by too low temperatures.

Salvia x superba 'MAY NIGHT'

Scabiosa caucasica

SCABIOUS, PINCUSHION FLOWER

ABOVE CLUMPS OF finely cut, grey-green foliage, scabious (*Scabiosa caucasica*) sends up stalks of blue, lavender-blue or white, 2–3-in (5–7.5-cm), richly textured flowers throughout the summer that are excellent for cutting. It grows 12–18 in (30–45 cm) tall, and is best enjoyed when planted in groups of three near the front of beds and borders. The best cultivar is 'Fama', with intense blue flowers on sturdy stems 18–24 in (45–60 cm) tall.

■ **CULTIVATION AND CARE TIPS.** It is easily grown in full sun with sandy to average, neutral to alkaline, well-drained soil. It does not do well under very hot conditions, unless grown in light shade. Set plants 12 in (30 cm) apart. Hardy to −40°F (−40°C). Deadhead regularly to prolong blooming.

■ **PROPAGATION.** Division in spring, if necessary. Fresh seed sown in autumn.

■ **PESTS AND DISEASES.** Slugs; snails; mildew.

Sedum 'AUTUMN JOY'

SEDUM

STONECROP

AN ENORMOUS GROUP of plants with hundreds of species, varieties, and cultivars, stonecrops are noted for their handsome succulent foliage, their showy, butterfly-attracting, long-lasting clusters of ¼-in (6-mm) flowers, and, particularly, their drought tolerance. Many are creeping plants especially good for rock gardens, draping over walls and steps, or edging paths. Taller types, growing to 2 ft (60 cm), are handsome additions to the middle of beds and borders.

■ **SPECIES, VARIETIES AND CULTIVARS.** The most widely grown stonecrop is the hybrid 'Autumn Joy' (also called 'Indian Chief'). Growing 2 ft (60 cm) tall with grey-green leaves, flowering starts in early autumn with the clusters of tiny flowers opening pale pink; gradually they deepen to salmon rose-red, then coppery bronze by late autumn and winter. These can be used in dried bouquets or left on for landscape interest in the winter. It is tolerant of moist soil and light shade, but does best in full sun with well-drained soil. Its parent

is the showy stonecrop (*Sedum spectabile*), which grows 2 ft (60 cm) tall with pink flowers. October daphne (*S. sieboldii*) is a trailing 6-in (15-cm) plant with semi-evergreen grey leaves and pink flowers in late autumn.

The purple-leaved great stonecrop (*S. maximum* 'Atropurpureum') sprawls stiffly with 2-ft (60-cm) stems; it has red-purple foliage and pink flowers in early autumn. Aizoon stonecrop (*S. aizoon*) grows 12–18 in (30–45 cm) tall with bright green leaves on erect stems and yellow flowers in summer. *S. kamtschaticum* grows 6–12 in (15–30 cm) tall with upright stems and yellow-orange flowers from midsummer until autumn.

■ **CULTIVATION AND CARE TIPS.** Tough, adaptable and easily grown, they tolerate a wide range of conditions, but do best in full sun and any well-drained soil. Set shorter types 12 in (30 cm) apart and taller ones 18–24 in (45–60 cm) apart. Hardy to −30°F (−34°C).

■ **PROPAGATION.** Division in spring. Cuttings in summer.

■ **PESTS AND DISEASES.** Rust.

Sedum kamtschaticum

Smilacina racemosa

SMILACINA

FALSE SOLOMON'S SEAL

asalse solomon's seal (*Smilacina racemosa*) has 18–36-in (45–60-cm) arching stems of pointed oval leaves resembling Solomon's seal. The flowers, produced in late spring, are 4–6-in (10–15-cm) feathery clusters of tiny creamy-white blooms, that, in late summer, become clusters of bright red berries. False Solomon's seal is a good foliage plant for naturalizing in light to full shade, spreading by thick rhizomatous roots, and is especially effective interplanted with spring-blooming bulbs or ferns, or planted either behind hostas or in front of shade-loving shrubs.

■ **CULTIVATION AND CARE TIPS.** It grows best in slightly acid, humus-rich, moist but well-drained soil. Space 12–18 in (30–45 cm) apart. Hardy to −30°F (−34°C).

■ **PROPAGATION.** Division in spring, which is seldom necessary except for increase. Seed sown in autumn.

■ **PESTS AND DISEASES.** Seldom bothered.

SOLIDAGO

GOLDEN ROD

Forming broad, upright clumps 18–42 in (45 cm–1.05 m) tall with branching, graceful golden-yellow flowers, golden rod blooms from midsummer into fall. The flowers are good for fresh arrangements as well as dried or preserved in glycerine for winter bouquets. Plant in the middle of beds and borders, mass in drifts or naturalize in meadow gardens. They can be really stunning if planted in groups of three. Given rich soil, the roots spread rapidly, and some types self-sow. In the wild, there are a number of species of golden rod, which readily hybridize, so specific identification is complicated and plants started from seed are variable. Buying named cultivars from nurseries is the best way to get better-flowering forms.

■ **CULTIVATION AND CARE TIPS.** It is very easily grown in full sun and almost any well-drained soil ranging from sandy to average. Light shade is tolerated. Set plants 18 in (45 cm) apart. Hardy to −30°F (−34°C).

■ **PROPAGATION.** Division in spring every three years.

■ **PESTS AND DISEASES.** Caterpillars; mildew.

Solidago

Stachys macrantha

STACHYS

BIG BETONY, LAMB'S TONGUE

THE TWO FORMS OF stachys useful in the garden are very dissimilar. Big betony (*Stachys macrantha*, also listed as *Betonica grandiflora*) has hairy, dark green, heart-shaped leaves that are wrinkled with scalloped edges. In late spring and early summer, whorled spikes of 1½-in (4-cm) violet, lavender-pink, or rosy pink flowers reach 18–24 in (45–60 cm) tall. Plant in at the front of beds and borders and use the flowers for cutting. Lamb's tongue (*S. byzantina*, also listed as *S. 'Olympica lanata'*) forms 2-ft (60-cm) ground-hugging mats of 4–6-in (10–15-cm) long white, thick, softly furry leaves with 12–18-in (30–5-cm) spikes of ½-in (12-mm) magenta flowers. The flowers are produced intermittently all summer; some gardeners prefer to cut them off to improve appearance and prevent self-sowing. This long-lived species makes a dense ground cover accent for the front of beds and borders, in a rock garden, or as an edging.

■ **CULTIVATION AND CARE TIPS.** Both forms grow well in poor to average, well-drained soils. Plant big betony in full sun to light shade and lamb's tongue in full sun. Set plants 12 in (30 cm) apart. Hardy to −30°F (−34°C).

■ **PROPAGATION.** Division in spring or autumn, every fourth year or when plants die out in the centre. Seed.

■ **PESTS AND DISEASES.** Seldom bothered, except lamb's tongue may rot in hot, humid climates.

Stachys byzantina

Stokesia laevis

STOKESIA

STOKES' ASTER

STOKES' ASTER (*Stokesia laevis*) forms stiff, branching plants with long, narrow leaves that are evergreen in warmer climates. Flowers are lacy, fringed, blue or white, and 4 in (10 cm) across on 12–24-in (30–60-cm) stems. Excellent for cutting, it is at its best planted in groups of three at the front of the border.

■ **CULTIVATION AND CARE TIPS.** Long-lived, it grows well in full sun with average, well-drained soil. Poor drainage in winter is usually fatal. Set plants 12–18 in (30–45 cm) apart. Deadhead regularly to prolong blooming. Hardy to −20°F (−28°C), with a loose winter mulch beneficial in colder areas to prevent roots heaving out of the ground.

■ **PROPAGATION.** Division in spring every four years. Seed.

■ **PESTS AND DISEASES.** Seldom bothered.

THALICTRUM

MEADOW RUE

AIRY CLOUDS OF LAVENDER, yellow or pink flowers above delicate blue-green leaves give meadow rues an elegant, fine-textured appearance that enhances the back of beds and borders, banks of streams or wildflower gardens. The flowers are good for cutting.

■ **SPECIES, VARIETIES AND CULTIVARS.** Columbine meadow rue (*Thalictrum aquilegifolium*) grows 3 ft (90 cm) tall with columbine-like leaves. Branching, crowded clusters of powderpuff-like, ½-in (12-mm) lavender flowers bloom in late spring. Lavender mist meadow rue (*T. rocquebrunianum*) grows 3–5 ft (90 cm–1.5 m) tall with leaves resembling maidenhair fern. The loose, open flower clusters, blooming in summer, are composed of ½-in (12-mm), five-petalled, purple or pink-lavender blooms centred with bright yellow stamens. Yellow meadow rue (*T. flavum*) grows 3–5 ft (90 cm–1.5 m) tall with masses of fluffy yellow flowers in summer.

■ **CULTIVATION AND CARE TIPS.** In cool-summer climates, they grow well in full sun but in hotter areas, light shade and a summer mulch is preferred. Provide humus-rich, moist but well-drained soil. Staking is necessary for lavender mist and yellow meadow rues. Set plants 18–24 in (45–60 cm) apart, preferably in groups of three. Plants take several years to become established. Hardy to −20°F (−28°C).

■ **PROPAGATION.** Division every four or five years in spring. Fresh seed sown in the autumn.

■ **PESTS AND DISEASES.** Seldom bothered.

Thalictrum flavum

Thermopsis villosa

THERMOPSIS

CAROLINA THERMOPSIS

RESEMBLING LUPIN, Carolina thermopsis (*Thermopsis villosa*, also listed as *T. caroliniana*) has 8–12-in (20–30-cm) long spikes of ½-in (12-mm) yellow, pea-like flowers on stout stalks 3–5 ft (90 cm–1.5 m) tall in early to midsummer. Plants slowly spread to form clumps 3 ft (90 cm) across. Long-lived, even surviving neglect, it has foliage attractive all summer long and deep, drought-resistant roots. Use at the back of borders or the centre of beds as well as in a meadow garden. The flowers are long-lasting in arrangements if cut when only the bottom flowers are open.

■ **CULTIVATION AND CARE TIPS.** It grows easily in poor to average, well-drained soil in full sun, although light shade is tolerated. Staking may be necessary with older plants or in windy sites. Set plants 2–3 ft (60–90 cm) apart. Hardy to −40°F (−40°C).

■ **PROPAGATION.** Division is seldom necessary and difficult because of the deep roots. Cuttings in late spring. Fresh seed sown in late summer.

■ **PESTS AND DISEASES.** Seldom bothered.

SPIDERWORT

LONG AND NARROW, the graceful, grasslike leaves of spiderwort (*T. × andersoniana*, also listed as *T. virginiana*) form robust clumps 2–3 ft (60–75 cm) tall. At intervals along the stems, clusters of three-petalled flowers, 1 in (2.5 cm) or more across, bloom throughout summer, with each flower lasting a day. A number of cultivars provide colours in shades of blue, pink, mauve, maroon, rose-purple, or white. Use spiderworts in beds and borders or naturalistic woodland gardens.

■ **CULTIVATION AND CARE TIPS.** Durable, long-lived plants, tolerating a wide range of conditions, it easily grows in full sun to light shade and poor to average, well-drained soil. Trimming stems to the ground in midsummer encourages new growth and autumn flowering. Set plants 18 in (45 cm) apart. Hardy to −30°F (−34°C).

■ **PROPAGATION.** Division in spring or autumn, as needed to control.

■ **PESTS AND DISEASES.** Slugs.

Tradescantia x andersoniana

Veronica teucrium 'CRATER LAKE BLUE'

VERONICA

SPEEDWELL, VERONICA

The growth habit of speedwells ranges from low, creeping forms to upright, bushy types, but all have pointed spikes of flowers in shades of blue as well as purple, pink, red or white that are excellent for cutting. Many kinds are low-maintenance perennials with a long blooming period, suitable either for the front or middle of beds and borders.

■ **SPECIES, VARIETIES AND CULTIVARS.** One of the best is 'Crater Lake Blue', a cultivar of Hungarian speedwell (*V. latifolia*, also listed as *V. teucrium*). Somewhat sprawling, it has ½-in (12-mm) navy blue flowers in late spring and early summer on plants 12 in (30 cm) tall with narrow, dark green, toothed leaves. Low-growing, woolly speedwell (*V. incana*) has silver-gray leaves on 6-in (15-cm) clumps and 12–18-in (30–45-cm) stems of ¼-in (6-mm) lilac-blue flowers in summer.

The best form of the beach, or clump, speedwell is *V. longifolia* 'Subsessilis'. It forms clumps of strong 2-ft (60-cm) stems with toothed, pointed leaves and densely packed spires of ½-in (12-mm) royal blue flowers bloom from midsummer to autumn. Spiked speedwell (*V. spicata*) grows 12–18 in (30–45 cm) tall with spikes of bright blue, ¼-in (6-mm) flowers during summer.

■ **CULTIVATION AND CARE TIPS.** Long-lived, they grow best in full sun, but tolerate light shade. Provide average, well-drained soil. Poorly drained soil in winter is often fatal. Remove faded flower spikes to prolong blooming. Set plants 12–18 in (30–45 cm) apart, singly or in groups of three. Hardy to −30°F (−34°C).

■ **PROPAGATION.** Division in spring or autumn every four years.

■ **PESTS AND DISEASES.** Powdery mildew.

VIOLA

VIOLET, PANSY, HEARTSEASE

DIMINUTIVE VIOLETS AND pansies have been grown and loved for centuries. Of the hundreds of species and many cultivars, some are weeds and other rare plants for the collector's garden. A few species can be singled out for use in front of beds and borders, in wild flower gardens, as a ground cover, or as an edging along paths. The flowers can be used in tiny bouquets.

■ **SPECIES, VARIETIES AND CULTIVARS.** Horned, or tufted, violet (*V. cornuta*) forms neat plants 6–8 in (15–20 cm) tall with 1-in (2.5 cm) violet, maroon, apricot, purple, yelow, or white flowers produced all summer long in full sun in areas where summers are cool and moist. With a summer mulch and light shade plants grow and bloom well in hotter areas. Hardy to −10°F (−23°C). Marsh blue violet (*V. cucullata*) grows 1 ft (30 cm) tall and slowly forms large patches from the spreading rhizomatous roots. It blooms in late spring and early summer with ½-in (12-mm) flowers of differ-

ent colours depending on the cultivar. Hardy to −30°F (−34°C). Sweet violet (*V. odorata*) blooms in spring on 8-in (20-cm) plants that spread by long runners called stolons. The purple, white or deep rose flowers are usually less than 1 in (2.5 cm) across with a delicate scent. Hardy to −10°F (−23°C). Heartsease (*V. tricolor*) grows 12 in (30 cm) tall with ½-in (12-mm) tri-coloured purple, yellow and white flowers from spring through early summer on thin, sprawling stems. It is short-lived but readily reseeds and grows in both full sun and light shade. Hardy to −30°F (−34°C).

■ **CULTIVATION AND CARE TIPS.** Most types grow well in light shade, except as noted. Average to humus-rich, moist but well-drained soil is preferred. Set plants 12 in (30 cm) apart.

■ **PROPAGATION.** Seed. Division in spring.

■ **PESTS AND DISEASES.** Mosaic; leaf spot; rust.

Viola tricolor

DESCRIPTIVE AND CULTIVATION DATA CHART

COLOUR: B=blue; L=lavender; O=orange; P=pink; Pu=purple; R=red; W=white; Y=yellow.
BLOOM: Sp=spring; ESp=early spring; Su=summer; ESu=early summer; A=autumn; EA=early
autumn. SUN: FSun=full sun; LSh=light shade; FSh=full shade.
SOIL: A=average–moderately rich and well-drained; D=dry–dries quickly, even after a heavy
rain; M=moist but well-drained–constantly, evenly moist but never soggy.

GENUS	COLOUR	HEIGHT	BLOOM	SUN	SOIL	SPACING
Achillea	P/R/W/Y	18in–4ft/45cm–1.2m	Su	FSun	A/D	10–18in/25–45cm
Aconitum	B/L/Pu	3–4ft/90cm–1.2m	Su/EA	FSun/LSh	M	18in/45cm
Adenophora	B	2–3ft/60–90cm	Su	FSun/LSh	M	12in/30cm
Alchemilla	Y	12–18in/30–45cm	Sp/ESu	FSun/LSh	M	12in/30cm
Amsonia	B	2–3ft/60–90cm	Sp/ESu	FSun/LSh	A/D	18in/45cm
Anaphalis	W	2ft/60cm	Su	FSun/LSh	M	12in/30cm
Anchusa	B	18in–4ft/45cm–1.2m	Sp/ESu	FSun/LSh	A	18–24in/45–60cm
Anemone	P/Pu/R/W	1–4ft/30cm–1.2m	Sp or A	FSun/LSh	A/M	8–18in/20–45cm
Anthemis	Y	10–24in/25–60cm	Su	FSun	A/D	12–15in/30–38cm
Aquilegia	B/P/R/W/Y/Pu	1–3ft/30–90cm	Sp/ESu	FSun/LSh	A	12in/30cm
Arabis	W/P	8in/20cm	Sp	FSun	A/D	8–12in/20–30cm
Armeria	R/P/W	6–18in/15–45cm	Sp/ESu	FSun	A/D	8–12in/20–30cm
Artemisia	Foliage/W	1–6ft/30cm–1.8m	Su	FSun	A/D	12–24in/30–60cm
Aruncus	W	1–5ft/30cm–1.5m	Su	LSh	M	24–30in/60–75cm
Asarum	Foliage	6in/15cm	—	LSh/FSh	M	8–12in/20–30cm
Asclepias	O	2–3ft/60–90cm	Su	FSun	A/D	12in/30cm
Aster	B/P/Pu/R/W	6in–6ft/15cm–1.8m	Su/A	FSun	M	12–18in/30–45cm
Astilbe	P/R/W	1–4ft/30cm–1.2m	Su	LSh	M	12–18in/30–45cm
Aubrietia	Pu/L/P/R	6in/15cm	Sp	FSun/LSh	D	6–8in/15–20cm
Aurinia/Alyssum	Y	12in/30cm	Sp	FSun	A/D	8–12in/20–30cm
Baptisia	B	3–4ft/90cm–1.2m	ESu	FSun/LSh	A	2ft/60cm
Belamcanda	O	12–30in/30–75cm	Su	FSun/LSh	A	12in/30cm
Bellis	P/R/W	3–6in/7.5–15cm	Sp/ESu	FSun/LSh	M	6in/15cm
Bergenia	P/R/W	12in/30cm	Sp	FSun/LSh	A/M	12in/30cm
Brunnera	B	12–18in/30–45cm	Sp	FSun/LSh	M	12in/30cm
Campanula	B/W/P/Pu	6in–5ft/15cm–1.5m	Su/A	FSun/LSh	A/M	10–24in/25–60cm
Centaurea	B/Pu/Y/W/P	2–4ft/60cm–1.2m	Sp/Su	FSun	A	18in/45cm
Centranthus	R/P/W	3ft/90cm	Su	FSun/LSh	A	12–18in/30–45cm
Cerastium	W	6in/15cm	ESu	FSun	A/D	12in/30cm
Chrysanthemum	L/O/P/Pu/R/W/Y	1–4ft/30cm–1.2m	LSu/A	FSun	A	12–18in/30–45cm
Chrysogonum	Y	4–6in/10–15cm	Sp/ESu	LSh/FSh	M	12in/30cm
Cimicifuga	W	2–8ft/60cm–2.4m	Su	FSun/FSh	M	2ft/60cm
Clematis	B/L/W	2–5ft/60cm–1.5m	Su	FSun/LSh	M	18in/45cm
Coreopsis	Y	6–30in/15–75cm	Su/A	FSun	A	12in/30cm
Delphinium	B/L/P/Pu/W	1–6ft/30cm–1.8m	Su	FSun/LSh	M	12–30in/30–75cm
Dianthus	P/R/W	6–18in/15–45cm	Sp/Su	FSun	A/D	8–12in/20–30cm
Dicentra	R/P/W	10–36in/25–90cm	Sp/Su	LSh/FSh	M	1–2ft/30–60cm
Dictamnus	W/P	2–3ft/60–90cm	ESu	FSun/LSh	M	3ft/90cm
Digitalis	P/R/W/Y	1–4ft/30cm–1.2m	ESu	FSun/LSh	M	12–16in/30–40cm
Doronicum	Y	12–30in/30–75cm	Sp/ESu	FSun/LSh	M	12in/30cm
Echinacea	P/W	2–4ft/60cm–1.2m	Su/A	FSun/LSh	A/D	18in/45cm
Echinops	B	3–5ft/90cm–1.5m	Su	FSun	A/D	18–24in/45–60cm
Erigeron	B/P/W/L	18–30in/45–75cm	Su	FSun/LSh	D	12in/30cm
Eryngium	B/W/L	1–4ft/30cm–1.2m	Su	FSun	D	1–2ft/30–60cm
Eupatorium	B/P	2–10ft/60cm–3m	Su/A	FSun	A/M	18–36in/45–90cm
Euphorbia	Y/R/W	6–36in/15–90cm	Sp/Su	FSun	D	12–18in/30–45cm

GENUS	COLOUR	HEIGHT	BLOOM	SUN	SOIL	SPACING
Ferns	Foliage	6in–6ft/15cm–1.8m		LSh/FSh	A/M	12–30in/30–75cm
Filipendula	P/W	18in–7ft/45cm–2.1m	Sp/Su	FSun/LSh	A/M	1–2ft/30–60cm
Gaillardia	O/R/Y	12–30in/30–75cm	Su/A	FSun	A/D	6–18in/15–45cm
Galium	Foliage/W	6–8in/15–20cm	Sp	LSh	M	12in/30cm
Geranium	L/P/Pu/W	6–24in/15–30cm	Sp/Su	FSun	A	12in/30cm
Geum	R/Y/O	1–2ft/30–60cm	Su	FSun/LSh	M	12–18in/30–45cm
Gypsophila	W/P	4in–3ft/10–90cm	Su	FSun	A	1–2ft/30–60cm
Helenium	R/Y/O	2–6ft/60cm–1.8m	Su/A	FSun	M	18–24in/45–60cm
Heliopsis	Y	2–6ft/60cm–1.8m	Su/A	FSun	A/M	2ft/60cm
Helleborus	W/P/Pu	1–2ft/30–60cm	ESp	FSun/LSh	M	18in/45cm
Hemerocallis	Y/O/P/R/Pu	1–6ft/30cm–1.8m	Su/A	FSun/LSh	A/M	1–2ft/30–60cm
Hesperis	P/Pu/W	2–3ft/60–90cm	Sp/ESu	FSun/LSh	M	18in/45cm
Heuchera	R/P/W	1–2ft/30–60cm	Su/A	FSun/LSh	M	12in/30cm
Hibiscus	R/P/W	2–8ft/60cm–2.4m	Su/A	FSun	M	3ft/90cm
Hosta	Pu/L/W/Foliage	6in–3ft/15–90cm	Su/A	LSh/FSh	M	1–2ft/30–60cm
Iberis	W	6–10in/15–25cm	Sp	FSun	M	15in/38cm
Iris	All colours	6in–4ft/15cm–1.2m	Sp/Su	FSun/LSh	A/M	12–18in/30–45cm
Kniphofia	O/R/Y	1–4ft/30cm–1.2m	Su	FSun	M	18in/45cm
Lavandula	L/Pu/P/W	1–3ft/30–90cm	Su	FSun	A/D	12in/30cm
Liatris	P/Pu/W	18in–5ft/45cm–1.5m	Su/A	FSun	A/M	12–18in/30–45cm
Linum	B/W/Y	1–2ft/30–60cm	Su	FSun	A/M	18in/45cm
Lobelia	R/B/Pu	2–4ft/60cm–1.2m	Su/A	LSh	M	12–18in/30–45cm
Lupinus	B/P/Pu/R/W/Y	2–3ft/60–90cm	ESu	FSun/LSh	M	18–24in/45–60cm
Lychnis	O/Pu/W/R	1–3ft/30–90cm	Su	FSun	A	12in/30cm
Lysimachia	W/Y	18–36in/45–90cm	Su	FSun/LSh	M	18–24in/45–60cm
Lythrum	P/Pu	30in–4ft/75cm–1.2m	Su/A	FSun	M	18in/45cm
Macleaya	W	6–10ft/1.8–3m	Su	FSun	A	3–4ft/90cm–1.20m
Marrubium	W	2–3ft/60–90cm	Su	FSun	A/D	12in/30cm
Mertensia	B/P/W	1–2ft/30–60cm	Sp	LSh	M	8–12in/20–30cm
Monarda	P/Pu/R/W	2–4ft/60cm–1.2m	Su	FSun/LSh	A/M	18in/45cm
Nepeta	B/W	12–18in/30–45cm	Sp/ESu	FSun	A/D	12–18in/30–45cm
Oenothera	Y/P	1–2ft/30–60cm	Su	FSun	A	18in/45cm
Orn. Grasses	Tan/W/Foliage	8in–6ft/20cm–1.8m	Su/A	FSun/LSh	A/M	1–2ft/30–90cm
Paeonia	P/R/W	2–3ft/60–90cm	LSp/ESu	FSun	M	2–3ft/60–90cm
Papaver	O/R/P/W	2–4ft/60cm–1.2m	ESu	FSun	A	18in/45cm
Phlox	P/Pu/R/W/B	6in–4ft/15cm–1.2m	Sp/A	FSun/LSh	M	1–2ft/30–60cm
Physostegia	P/L/W	2–4ft/60cm–1.2m	Su/A	FSun	A/M	18–24in/45–60cm
Platycodon	B/P/W	18–30in/45–75cm	Su	FSun/LSh	A/D	12–18in/30–45cm
Polygonatum	W	1–6ft/30cm–1.8m	Sp	LSh/FSh	M	18–24in/45–60cm
Primula	B/L/Pu/R/W/Y	6–24in/15–60cm	Sp/ESu	LSh	M	12in/30cm
Pulmonaria	B/P/W	6–18in/15–45cm	Sp	LSh	M	12in/30cm
Rudbeckia	Y	2–6ft/60cm–1.8m	Su/A	FSun	A/M	18in/45cm
Salvia	B/Pu/P	18–36in/45–90cm	Su	FSun	A	12–18in/30–45cm
Scabiosa	B/L/W	1–2ft/30–60cm	Su/A	FSun	A/D	12in/30cm
Sedum	P/R/W/Y	4–24in/10–60cm	Su/A	FSun	A/D	1–2ft/30–60cm
Smilacina	W	18–36in/45–90cm	Sp	LSh/FSh	M	12–18in/30–45cm
Solidago	Y	18–42in/45cm–1.05m	Su/A	FSun	A/D	18in/45cm
Stachys	Foliage/L/P/Pu	8–24in/20–60cm	Su	FSun/LSh	A/D	12in/30cm
Stokesia	B/W	1–2ft/30–60cm	Su/A	FSun	A	12–18in/30–45cm
Thalictrum	L/P/Y	3–5ft/90cm–1.5m	Sp/Su	FSun/LSh	M	18–24in/45–60cm
Thermopsis	Y	3–5ft/90cm–1.5m	ESu	FSun	A/D	2–3ft/60–90cm
Tradescantia	B/P/Pu/R/W	24–30in/60–75cm	Su	FSun/LSh	A/D	18in/45cm
Veronica	B/P/Pu/R/W	6–24in/15–60cm	Su	FSun	A	12–18in/30–45cm
Viola	B/Pu/O/R/W/Y	6–12in/15–30cm	Sp/A	FSun/FSh	A/M	12in/30cm

INDEX

Numbers in italics refer to illustration captions